EVERY DIAMOND
DOESN'T SPARKLE

EVERY DIAMOND
DOESN'T SPARKLE

by FRESCO THOMPSON

Written with CY RICE

DAVID McKAY COMPANY, INC.

New York

EVERY DIAMOND DOESN'T SPARKLE

COPYRIGHT © 1964 BY FRESCO THOMPSON AND CY RICE

LIBRARY OF CONGRESS CATALOG CARD NUMBER: 64-20243

MANUFACTURED IN THE UNITED STATES OF AMERICA

VAN REES PRESS • NEW YORK

To the gentlemen in blue, the umpires, without whose integrity and devotion to their assigned tasks this great game of baseball would not be possible.

My dedication of this book to the umpires may come as a shock to those arbiters who umpired when I was a player or manager. I antagonized and needled more than my share of umpires, but as I questioned their eyesight and became mystified at what they saw, I always respected their honesty.

FOREWORD

LAFAYETTE FRESCO THOMPSON has been a valuable member of the Dodger organization since 1940. His position with us is Vice President and Director of Dodger Minor League Clubs. That's a pretty long title. It can be shortened to Talent Boss.

There have been many famous voices in baseball heard from the dugouts, coaching boxes, front offices, but none have crackled with quicker wit and richer humor than Fresco's. No newspaperman ever interviewed him without coming away with a few original lines that made readers chuckle in the next edition.

He can dish out a joke and take one on himself. He still laughs at the time some Pittsburgh scribe scribbled, "Lafayette Fresco Thompson and all his names were released outright to Buffalo today."

That Fresco's mind never wanders from baseball was exemplified one cold, blustery day back in Brooklyn when he entered a department store to buy something to keep his hands warm.

"Good afternoon, sir," the salesman greeted. "What do you have in mind?"

"Gloves," Thompson said.

"What kind, sir?"

"Infielders'," slipped out of Fresco.

Fresco knocked off a year from his age when he started to play baseball. "But," he says, "I rapidly gained it back during the worrying stages of building Dodger Stadium in Los Angeles."

His daughter Ann once asked him to read a school lesson she was preparing, in which the child was asked to name the most pleasant sound, odor, taste, and sight she had ever experienced. She showed her parent what she had written, questioning, "Daddy, is that what you'd put?"

Fresco said, "Yes," because of not wishing to confuse the young academic mind.

"I guess I didn't really tell the child the truth," he told his wife Peg after Ann had gone to bed. "For sound—it would be the crack of a bat hitting a ball; odor—the locker room after a game; taste—victory; sight—the Dodgers beating the Giants."

Fresco lost his voice cheering when we defeated the Yankees four straight in the 1963 World Series. That's the only thing he ever lost as long as he's been with us. Throughout the years he's gained in business acumen, enthusiasm, priceless humor. His loyalty to the organization is deep-rooted as a California redwood. His memory is photographic when it comes to assimilating a record book. He knows the history of baseball from A to Z. He'd tell you the A would stand for Alexander, Grover Cleveland, pitcher (1909-1930), and the Z for Zachary, Tom, pitcher (1918-1936).

When baseball greats are mentioned you never hear the name of Fresco Thompson. Mostly it's the sluggers and pitchers who have made the Hall of Fame who are remembered. Yet in playing minor and major league ball for seventeen years he had a .302 batting average.

There was one department not contained in the records in which he topped them all: silencing hecklers. His caustic ad libs singed the ears of many a dissenting fan and opposing player.

Fresco Thompson loves baseball with a fierce and burning intensity. He can view a doubleheader, stop en route home and watch two pick-up teams playing in a park, eat dinner and settle down with the *Sporting News,* his bible. And when he falls asleep that night, it's a safe bet to assume that in a dream he hit a home run with the bases loaded in the last half of the ninth.

He's a Dodger at heart—a very valuable and trusted one—and he always will be.

WALTER O'MALLEY

CONTENTS

xi

EVERY DIAMOND
DOESN'T SPARKLE

CHAPTER 1

HOW DAFFY WERE THE DODGERS?

As far as I was concerned, 1916 was an ideal year for my family to move to New York City. The schools were closed due to an infantile paralysis epidemic. Every morning I left home carrying a baseball glove in my hand and ten cents in my pocket given me by Mother for lunch. The money bought a glass of lemonade from a pushcart and a hot dog dripping with sauerkraut.

Some kids wore bags of camphor around their necks; others had sacks of asafetida, or sassafras, or onions. These amulets, parents thought, protected their offspring against the dreaded disease.

I wore no charms.

My father explained to my mother why it wasn't necessary. He related, "The way that boy is swinging his bat and striking out, he's apt to club any stray germs to death."

What Dad had said popped into my mind as I stood at the plate at Ebbets Field in 1931 wearing a Brooklyn Dodger uniform, trying to solve the slants of hurler Carl Hubbell. Trotting out to play second base, I kept thinking, The adventure's on the field, but security for a baseball career man is located in the front office.

Reaching the portals of that office took seven years of struggling up a twisting pathway through promotional work, major league scouting, minor league field management. Today I occupy a smartly appointed office in the nation's most beautiful stadium. My title is Vice President and Director of Dodger Minor League Clubs, a string of farm teams operating in various cities where future diamond stars just beginning to twinkle are toiling, hoping some day to negotiate the giant jump to the parent club.

Clubs under my supervision are Spokane, Pacific Coast League; Albuquerque, Texas League; Salem, Northwest League; Grand Forks, Northern League; Santa Barbara, California League; Salisbury, Western Carolinas League; and St. Petersburg, Florida, Florida State League.

Sometimes I sit on a tribunal with Buzzie Bavasi and Al Campanis, discussing and figuring advantageous trades. On one point we've always agreed: none of us would trade our own jobs with anybody else. We're all happy.

Baseball has been my life and it's given me as full and rich a life as I could ask for. During high school and college days at Columbia University I lived practically in the shadow of the Polo Grounds. Days when no game was scheduled I'd climb Coogan's Bluff, which was comparable to Mount Olympus, and gaze reverently at the empty stands. When the action was taking place I often sat on the Bluff and from this lofty position could look through slits in the grandstand and watch players in two positions— second base and right field. I was privileged to see Larry Doyle and Benny Kauff and follow their movements, trying to piece together the puzzle of who was on what base.

Not too many years later I was brought up from Buffalo in the International League to play for the Giants under tough John McGraw. Only two weeks remained in the season and McGraw decided to start me along with Al Moore and "Blackie" Carter, both rookies like myself. McGraw figured it was pretty safe to start us. No matter how lousy we might play it was impossible to damage the standing of the team.

Moore, Carter, and I took batting practice with McGraw eagle-eyeing us behind the cage. Balls were sailing 340 to 345 feet into the outfield at the Polo Grounds for what would have been lazy fly balls, when McGraw barked, "I guess those are home runs in that jerk league you guys just came out of."

No one answered.

The Giants won the game 3 to 2 and we rookies got five of the team's six hits. Afterwards the players were undressing in the clubhouse. The rookies hung their clothes on rusty nails instead of in the steel lockers used by the veterans. You could almost get tetanus while dressing. Later I thought it might have been better if I had.

I said cockily to those within listening range, "Those damned Giants would have been in a helluva fix if it wasn't for those jerk leaguers today."

Hardly were the words out of my mouth than the rasping voice of McGraw retorted, "My boy, one small breeze doesn't make a windstorm."

My baseball career reads like a geography lesson. I played at Uniontown, Alabama; Grand Island, Nebraska; Omaha, Nebraska; Montreal; Minneapolis; Kansas City; Buffalo; Pittsburgh with the Pirates; New York with the Giants; and Philadelphia with the Phillies.

3

And finally the Dodger organization, but this wasn't the end of the trail.

I've had but two true loves in my life: my wife and baseball. Both have been served faithfully. My wife Peggy is a ball fan with certain reservations. She knows there are nine men on a team, but always presumed the other eight were present only to assist me.

Our love survived a stern test. On the first day of the World Series we left on our honeymoon in the Adirondacks. I never found out who won the game until noon of the next day.

I can best compare my many years with the Dodgers to being a voyager on the high seas of baseball. It was analogous to embarking on four cruises with four different skippers at the helm.

First was Uncle Wilbert Robinson.

Second was Larry MacPhail.

Third was Branch Rickey.

Fourth and current is Walter O'Malley.

The tenure with Robinson was akin to being aboard a floating insane asylum minus a compass; with MacPhail, caught in a ground swell near a rocky coastline; with Rickey, placid under fair skies; with O'Malley, constant threat of rough water.

Four more diversified personalities never existed.

The Brooklyn Dodgers were created in 1883, which makes them older than Warren Spahn. The name was derived from Trolley Dodgers, an appellation applied to inhabitants of Brooklyn who were busy running a broken field across intersections to avoid being bludgeoned by cowcatchers on streetcars. Other titles they selected were Robins, Bridegrooms (which lasted six months, to be

4

changed to Superbas—a name sounding too much like a cigar) and then back to just plain Dodgers.

There was nothing plain about the Dodgers when I reported to their fold. The transition in miles was negligible. All I did was cross the Brooklyn Bridge after taking the train from Philadelphia. Although I had spent many years in Manhattan, Brooklyn, despite the fact it was a borough, seemed remote as Central Africa to me. We seldom went to Brooklyn unless we happened to fall asleep on the subway.

Uncle Robbie, since 1914, had managed the team. He was of the old school who left an imprint on baseball that the modern manager doesn't. Men like John McGraw, Kid Gleason, Hughie Jennings, Pat Moran, or Connie Mack were at the helm of the same club from ten to twenty years. They had a Siamese-twin-like relationship with their club. They had an identity.

Such doesn't exist in modern-day baseball. Managers play musical chairs, jumping from one job to another. Charley Dressen, presently managing Detroit, was at Brooklyn, Cincinnati, and Washington. Bobby Bragan, at Milwaukee, called the shots for Cleveland and Pittsburgh. The Reds' Freddie Hutchinson held the reins of the Cardinals and Detroit. Before Lou Boudreau reached Kansas City he first stopped at Cleveland and Boston. Jimmy Dykes, the most traveled of them all, directed the destinies of the White Sox, Phillies, Baltimore, Detroit, Cincinnati, and Cleveland. Their lives and railroad tickets bore a similarity.

Robbie was one of the old Baltimore Orioles, that great team upon whose roster was John McGraw and other legendary names. Baltimore, of course, is still called the

5

Orioles, but the birds don't fly into the same high altitude they once did.

Robbie was a roly-poly, genial, jolly fellow weighing 300 pounds. When his dentures fitted properly you could even understand him. He missed by many miles being a baseball genius, and his arch rival and hated enemy, John McGraw, could have stayed in bed the afternoon of a Dodger-Giant fracas and still outsmarted him.

I had joined the Phillies and played with them in 1927, 1928, 1929, and 1930, captaining them for the last two and one-half years. In my initial year Stuffy McInnis, the first sacker of Connie Mack's $100,000 infield of the early days, managed us, later to be replaced by Burt Shotton, who in turn handled the Dodgers.

In 1929, the year the stock market went down, our batting averages went up. I hit .324, got 202 base hits, yet my average was sixth on the club. Bill Terry led the league with .401. The only fellow among the regulars I outhit was Tommy Thevenow, and everyone always outhit Tommy. We boasted sluggers like Lefty O'Doul, .398; Chuck Klein, .360; Don Hurst, .340; Spud Davis, .330; and Pinky Whitney, .325.

I'm lucky the bat boy didn't play or he might have outhit me. We could belt the cover off the ball, but due to poor pitching, were a fixture in the tail-end position.

The Phils in those days were known as the "Phutile Phils" and there was a cliché going around the City of Brotherly Love that on a clear day they could see seventh place. I played for them in the B.M. period—which doesn't mean what it implies. It meant Before Money. Every time we had a payday we had to sell a ballplayer. We'd get beat 7-6, 8-7, 12-11. While we couldn't seem to kick the extra point, we had no trouble kicking the ball around.

The Phillies' ball park was a diminutive one and they used to say that the right field fence was so short that lefthanded pitchers couldn't throw sidearm because they'd scrape their knuckles against the boards.

Right field sported a huge red-painted sign advertising LIFEBUOY SOAP in block letters and underneath proclaimed: "The Phillies Use Lifebuoy Soap." One afternoon we came out to the park and found that someone had sneaked in the evening before and, using a large brush and can of white paint, printed in two-foot-high letters under the slogan: AND THEY STILL STINK!

Tom Meany, an astute sports and magazine writer, invited me to a Knights of Columbus dinner at the Columbus Council in Brooklyn, to tag along with him and say a few words. When it came my time to speak Tom introduced me as the new Dodger second baseman who had just been traded from the Phillies where he was captain. In his remarks Tom said that being captain of the Phillies had the same prestige as that of being a WPA foreman.

Meany was on the staff of the *New York World-Telegram* along with such notables of the typewriter as Joe Williams, Heywood Broun, Westbrook Pegler, Tim Cohane. After a stint with this paper he became sports editor of the now defunct *Collier's*.

Soon after assuming his position he was handed an assignment by the magazine. He called his wife and instructed, "Clara, I want you to pack a bag for me, I have to make a trip."

She asked, "Where are you going?"

7

"To Puerto Rico," Tom said.

"Oh," she exclaimed, "that's a switch. I thought they always came here."

Ebbets Field had an intimacy found in no other ball park. Playing the infield you experienced the same feeling you'd have if you were entertaining thousands of unruly people in the sitting room of your home. If a fan whispered, it traveled nearly to second base and what reached your ears wasn't exactly music if someone called you a bum. As any visitor to Brooklyn soon learns, few residents of that borough whisper, so we didn't miss much in the infield. One day at second base I heard a fan discussing his wife's infidelities.

Marconi invented the wireless (radio), but Brooklyn Dodger fans went a step further scientifically. To each game they carried a built-in public address system—needing no batteries—in their larynxes. Amplified were Bronx cheers, boos, catcalls, assorted invectives. A Bronx cheer originating from the lips and tongues of Brooklynites cannot be duplicated. Perhaps the fans hold patent rights. It has a wet, clinging consistency, drenching the victim with insult.

While on the subject of public address systems, the head man of ours was an announcer named Ricketts. This was in the heyday of Tex Rickard the promoter, prompting everyone to call Ricketts "Tex." I recollect two of his most brilliant outpourings.

Into the mike he said, "Ladies and gentlemen, a little boy has been found lost."

When the sun beat down on Ebbets Field and the game progressed, many fans started divesting themselves of garments, beginning with coats, followed by neckties,

8

shirts, even shoes, often hanging these discards over the railings. The large-scale disrobing was the bane of the umpires' existence. They voiced strenuous objections because a ball could catch in the clothes and become a home run instead of bouncing back onto the playing field. This created a prime opportunity for Ricketts to sneak in a prize malapropism:

"The umpires request that the fans in the left field boxes will kindly remove their clothing."

Cool heads prevailed, preventing one of the most extensive mass strip acts in history.

Mistakes were so prolific that Uncle Robbie decided to form a Bonehead Club.

"It won't be very exclusive," he prophesied.

When someone asked, "Who'll be president?" Robbie stated, "Time will furnish the candidates."

Robbie appointed himself Treasurer and a supreme court of one to pass judgment on the severity of the boner and the levying of fines running up to five dollars.

He solemnly predicted: "If we continue as we are, we'll take all this money at the end of the season and have a party. It oughtta be one of the best parties anybody ever had. Why, it might even continue unabated until spring training."

The basic idea seemed sound. However, it proved unworkable.

Prior to a game with the Cards, managed by Frankie Frisch, Robbie announced in the clubhouse that Ernie Lombardi would catch. He made up a lineup and mistakenly put Al Lopez' name in to do the receiving. Lombardi was in the game, but had not been publicly announced; therefore, Robbie was subject to a fine and we couldn't use Lopey if we wanted to.

The Bonehead Club was quickly dissolved.

On the team we had a real character, a huge right-handed pitcher named Clarence "Pea Ridge" Day, who hailed from Pea Ridge, Arkansas. He was an accomplished hog caller, having won a number of contests in this guttural sport. His throat, many opined, was coated with highway pavement. Should Pea Ridge have a good inning and perhaps strike out a key man in a jam, on his way to the bench he'd favor the fans by an exhibition of his throaty cries that shook the foundations of the antiquated buildings around the ball park.

A powerful, barrel-chested individual, he could, merely by expansion, bust any baseball belt with his chest. Periodically players expressed doubts this feat could be accomplished by a mere mortal, backing their opinions by wagers that invariably found their way into the pockets of Pea Ridge.

Skeptics would personally adjust the belt tightly around the chest of the Arkansan, who huffed and puffed until his face changed from rosy red to blue—but net results were always the same: the buckle, the leather, the rivets flew all over the clubhouse.

As previously mentioned, Lefty O'Doul was on the club. Besides wielding a fantastic bat, Lefty was a shrewd diplomat, politician, schemer, and gagster. He concentrated on Pea Ridge, his nimble brain concocting a plan. From the equipment man he obtained a new belt made of heavy cowhide more than one-eighth of an inch thick. He took it to a harness maker. Under his guidance the harness maker reinforced the belt in every possible—yet concealing—way, substituting heavy copper rivets for the ordinary ones. O'Doul was ready for Pea Ridge.

Lefty started an argument, belittling Pea Ridge's belt-breaking abilities. After five minutes of caustic comments, a twenty dollar bet was placed. Considering Lefty had paid the harness maker only a dollar fifty, this would leave—if he won—a neat profit.

"Shucks," Pea Ridge mumbled, "it'll be the easiest money I ever made."

Lefty tightened the belt around Pea Ridge's chest. The hog caller inhaled, then expanded. Nothing happened. He tried it again. The rivets still held. Resting for a moment, he prepared for one last mighty effort. Again he failed, collapsing on the floor in pain. He had broken two ribs.

His hog calling days were temporarily ended.

"You sure took the wind out of his sails," complimented an admiring observer.

O'Doul gave a satisfied nod. "I not only took the wind out of his sails, I sank the boat."

Judge Kenesaw Mountain Landis, the Commissioner of Baseball, visited the Dodger camp at Clearwater, Florida. Soon after arrival he approached Pea Ridge Day.

"Mr. Day," Landis asked, "do you have any casualties?"

"No, Judge," Pea Ridge responded, "but we have two Poles and a Swede."

The daffiness of the Dodgers was not restricted to the playing field. John Gorman, general manager of the club, got into the act. We were in Chicago, stopping at the Edgewater Beach Hotel. One of our farm teams happened to be in Clinton, Iowa, a distance of about 120 miles from

11

the Windy City. Gorman had never visited a farm team. He decided to go see Clinton play.

He came down the hotel steps around mid-afternoon, climbed into a cab, and casually said, "Clinton."

"Whereabouts on Clinton you wanna go?" the driver questioned.

"Not a street—Clinton, Iowa," Gorman said, settling back in the seat for the long ride.

Upon arrival at the Clinton ball park, he discovered that instead of the game being played that night it had been shifted to a day game, and was already over. He left the park and outside the gate, on purely a hunch, the cab driver was waiting.

"Edgewater Beach Hotel?" he asked.

"Right," Gorman said, climbing in.

Having been a catcher, Robbie was, as all managers are, highly critical of a fellow playing his own position. After we lost to the Cubs in Chicago in the last inning on one pitch, Robbie asked Lopez, "What'd you call for?"

"Curve."

The answer mattered little. Robbie was in a castigating mood.

"A high school boy would have known better," he sputtered, to begin groaning, complaining and grumbling over Lopez' alleged stupidity.

Lopez took as much abuse as he could before he proposed, "Look, Robbie, if I'm so dumb, why don't you call all the signs? I'll look over at the bench and you give 'em to me."

Robbie's face brightened. "Why, I'll just do that."

The next day one of our aces was on the mound, Van Lingle Mungo. Pat Malone, a Cub dependable, opposed him. For three innings it was scoreless tie, with Robbie wigwagging signals from the bench. Lopez would go into his crouch and, before relaying the sign to Mungo, take a fast look at Robbie.

"See how easy it is," Robbie's voice floated the length of the bench.

Came the fourth inning The first Cub batter cracked a single to right; the next man walked; Mungo slipped and fell on a bunt and the bases were loaded, nobody out. Lopez went into his crouch, twisted his head, eyes searching for Robbie.

There was no sight of the manager. For the first three innings he had been easy to locate.

Lopez stood up, waited several seconds and again assumed his crouching position and looked for Robbie. The manager was still among the missing. One of the players on our bench yelled at Robbie, who was over at the drinking fountain cleaning tobacco from underneath his lower bridge:

"Hey, Robbie! Lopey wants you!"

Robbie kept on cleaning his bridge.

Now the entire bench took up the cry: "Robbie! Lopez wants you!"

Impatiently the umpire ordered the game to continue. Robbie adjusted the plate in his mouth, sauntered over to the front of the dugout and looked at his catcher. Lopez was standing, peering at him, hands spread beseechingly.

Cupping his hand, Robbie yelled, "What's the matter with you—didn't you ever catch before?"

We had a lefthanded slugger on the team named Babe Herman who still holds some of the Dodger records. He wielded a "seeing eye" bat. His lifetime average was around .365. In the trade we called Babe a "wood man," for he was strictly a hitter. Babe didn't worry much about his fielding. He wore a glove for only one reason: it was the league custom. The glove would last him a minimum of six years because it rarely made contact with a ball. Yet it did serve a purpose: On a chilly day at the beginning of the season it kept his right hand as warm as his left, which was in his pocket.

The year before I joined the Dodgers the team was making a good run for the pennant. When the Brooklyn team reached Cincinnati the Dodgers and the Reds were tied. Hollis Thurston, known as "Sloppy," now a scout for the Chicago White Sox, was pitching for Brooklyn against the Reds and leading 2 to 1 going into the last inning.

The Cincy batter smacked a line drive to right field which Herman, displaying his usual aplomb, played into a triple. It wasn't easy. But you could always depend on the Babe. Two runners crossed the plate and Brooklyn got beat 3 to 2.

The Cards won their game, pushing the Dodgers into second place. They were a pretty disconsolate bunch and everybody felt sympathy for Herman because he personally blew it. Herman, together with Glenn Wright and Thurston, piled into a cab bound for the Sinton Hotel where the team was staying.

The atmosphere inside the cab was funereal. There was no conversation. The whirring of the tires and the ticking of the meter were the only audible sounds. Thurston was mentally suffering after his bad luck in losing a tough one, and Glenn Wright, wondering if his chance at Series money had gone down the drain, wasn't doing much to brush aside the gloom. Herman buried his head in his hands. Pity flowed from Wright and Thurston toward the Babe.

Halfway to the hotel Herman broke the silence.

"Gee, fellows, you know, if that last ball I hit fell in there, I'd be hitting .370."

"Stop the cab!" Thurston bellowed.

The car came to a screeching halt in the middle of nowhere.

Thurston hopped out, explaining to Wright, "I wouldn't ride another foot with this guy, talking about how much he'd be hitting, when he just knocked us out of first place with his glove."

After I'd joined the Dodgers, Herman pulled another crazy boner against the Giants at the Polo Grounds. The game reached the final inning. The Dodgers were one run ahead, one out, but the Giants had a man on second. The next batter hit a fly ball into deep right field, which Herman backed up and caught for the second out. Much to everyone's astonishment, the Babe stuck the ball in his pocket and sprinted for the clubhouse, allowing the tying run to score.

The Babe had miscalculated—a not uncommon occurrence with him—thinking it was the third out and the game was over. Our two remaining fielders chased him into the clubhouse and brought him back to complete the game.

At spring training we were all out on the field and Thurston, glancing over at the gate leading from the clubhouse, spied the Babe and Lefty O'Doul, the two well-known "wood men," coming out carrying six bats apiece thrown over their shoulders.

He quipped, "Here come O'Doul and Herman for their fielding practice."

Herman and O'Doul babied their bats with loving care and affection. They'd go to a butcher and get a nice, long, fresh bone and bone their bats, nursing them and rubbing them and applying sandpaper. The bone prevented the bats from peeling, protected the grain, and hardened the wood.

At spring training down at Clearwater, Florida, we had such a large number of players it became necessary for our major-domo of the clubhouse, Dan Comerford, who was in charge of the equipment, to double up some of the players' lockers.

Comerford was a real oldtimer. He wore a celluloid collar large enough in diameter and wide enough to keep the score of a twelve inning game on before the figures met around the collar. The popular whiplash would be unknown if motorists wore such a collar today.

Dan assigned me to the same locker as Herman. I was getting dressed when he came in, spotted me, and boomed at Dan, "Hey! What's the idea of havin' me dressin' with a .250 hitter?"

I retorted, "*You* should feel bad! How do you think I feel dressing with a .250 fielder?"

That same year the Dodgers had signed a young graduate of Manhattan College. We were playing one day, with no chance of catching the opposition, and Uncle Robbie decided the time was appropriate to wet the newcomer's feet.

"Go out and play the eighth and ninth innings and get oriented," counseled Robbie, adding, "You'll get over some of your nervousness."

The recruit couldn't have had a more miserable inning. He misjudged a couple of fly balls, a grounder trickled between his legs, he tossed a ball into the dugout.

16

Robbie, softie and sentimentalist that he was, mused, "Maybe I shouldn't play this boy at home, but start him on the road." Turning to Casey Stengel, he ordered, "Go out and play right field the last inning."

Stengel trotted to his position and for everything the rookie did wrong, Casey did two things wrong. A ball streaked between his legs and as he turned to play the bounce off the fence, it came back through his legs again. Not only did he miss the same ball twice, but made a poor throw to the infield.

Stengel came into the dugout. Robbie walked up to him, demanding, "Case, what happened out there in right?"

"Well, Robbie, that damned collegian's got that out-field in such shape nobody could play it," Stengel said.

I recall another outfielder who had a bad day, but there were two people who might disagree. He was Heinie Mueller, a German boy from St. Louis, playing with the Cardinals. Two girl friends from his church came out to see him perform and, per usual whenever a ballplayer's friends were in the stands, it was an un-written guarantee of poor performance.

Heinie muffed two flies, was picked off first base, struck out twice. Fans were riding him. In the last inning Card manager Gabby Street, who once caught Walter Johnson and a ball dropped from the Washington Monument (if he caught one today he'd be signed for our space pro-gram), decided to put in a pinch hitter for Heinie. A utility infielder named Jake Flowers was sent to bat.

The park announcer, carrying a huge megaphone, bleated through it: "FLOWERS FOR MUELLER!"

One of Heinie's girl friends gurgled, "Isn't it wonder-ful to honor Heinie that way."

It seemed that when Uncle Robbie was managing the Dodgers everyone, not only in Brooklyn but in the entire City of New York, recognized him in public. Off the field, Ma Robinson, his wife, was constantly at his side, backing him in every decision he made—right or wrong—and defending him during the numerous arguments he had with cab drivers who tried to second-guess him.

Jolly old Robbie had once bade farewell to baseball for six years, to become a butcher and proprietor of a meat market. Six years of cutting, slicing, and trimming the fat off meat—something he couldn't do to his own waistline—were enough. He found scant exitement in wrapping a ham hock. The smell of a locker room after a game was a whiff of heaven, even when compared with the succulent odor of one of his own cooked prime ribs.

During 1932 his team for two and one-half months led the league, only to fall thuddingly on their collective rears in the stretch, ending fourth. They drew one million, one hundred thousand at home. In 1932 he was eased out of the organization after eighteen years.

None would forget him.

Robbie, a sympathetic soul, was extremely solicitous regarding the health of his players, constantly inquiring about their aches and pains and whether or not they were able to play on a particular day.

We were in St. Louis. It was mid-August, hot and humid. In the clubhouse prior to the game Robbie approached Captain Glenn Wright.

"Cap, you play a little shortstop for old Robbie today?"

Glenn pointed to his left ankle that had been sprained for three days. "I just can't put my weight on it. I don't believe I'd do the club any good."

Robbie shrugged. "That's alright, Cap, that's alright.

18

If you don't feel like playing we don't want you to get out there. We never want you out there if you aren't in good shape."

Turning to Oscar Slade, who was also a shortstop, he said, "How about you, Oz? Want to play a little shortstop for old Robbie?"

"Robbie, you know that knee I hurt when I ran into that tarpaulin in Cincy," Slade replied. "It's still giving me a lot of trouble. Bothers me a lot. Don't think I can get out there and play."

Robbie's head bobbed up and down. "Alright, alright. Don't want to play you unless you're in good shape."

His eyes fastened on Jake Flowers, a Cardinal acquisition who had been bothered by ulcers for the last few months, and asked, "How about you, Jake? Play a little shortstop for old Robbie today?"

Jake sighed. "Robbie, the heat here in St. Louis kept me up all night. Hardly closed my eyes. And my ulcers are giving me fits with this food on the road and I can't stick to my diet. My stomach is turning somersaults."

"Alright, Jake. That's alright," Robbie said, understandingly. "We don't want any sick boys playing."

Robbie looked up and down the bench, finally spotting me, and called, "How about you, Tommy? You want to play a little shortstop for old Robbie?"

I was his last hope.

"Well, Robbie," I said, "it's either you or me, and I wouldn't want you to get out there in that hot sun, so I'll do it for you."

We got started and I was fortunate; I didn't have too many plays. Tossing them for us was big John Picus Quinn, a righthanded spitballer. He really drowned a

19

baseball. The hide on the horse the ball came from had never been so clean when the animal was alive.

Quinn, a ripe forty-seven years of age, wasn't exactly a gazelle on the hill. He belonged to that venerable pitchers' union that called the dirt circling the mound the extent of their fielding range, and anything falling on the grass belonged to someone else.

Going into the eighth inning we led 4 to 3. They had a man on third, two down, and it was their pitcher's turn to bat. Andy High was sent in to pinch hit. Old John wound up and came sidearm with his best spitter. Reaching home plate, the ball broke in on Andy's fist and came almost directly back to Quinn. He was in a follow-through position and sort of raised his gloved hand a little over his shoulder, waving at the ball.

I came charging in. The ball went by John and I nailed it on the short hop, felt that I was lucky to come up with it, and drew back to throw. Just as I put the pressure on to get it over to first base, I felt the saliva spot John had put on the ball when he made his delivery.

I said to myself, "Look out, upper tier, here goes a wild throw." I tossed to first, giving it body English. Del Bissonette, stretching and straining, snagged the ball with the tip of his toe touching the bag. Andy High was out by half a split second.

Sitting down on the bench I remarked to Bissonette, "Del, that was *really* quite a play."

Overhearing the remark, Robbie spluttered, "Whatsa matter, whatsa matter, it was only a routine play—just stretched out and got the ball, that's all."

"I know, Robbie," I explained, "but just as I put the pressure on the ball before I threw it, I felt this spit and I was afraid I'd heave it away."

Robbie stared at me and inquired casually, "Why didn't you wipe it off?"

A silly question deserves a silly answer, so I retorted, "Well, Robbie, I was going to ask for a new ball but I couldn't find the umpire."

We were playing a game at Ebbets Field during my first season and the latter part of it we were trailing by a couple of runs. It was our pitcher's turn to bat. I leaned forward when I saw Robbie searching the bench for a pinch hitter, feeling I was the equal of anyone sitting there. Much to my surprise, Robbie called on Fred Heimach, a lefthanded pitcher who was a good clouter.

Heimach responded to Robbie's choice by singling sharply to center field. Fred being rather stoutish and no greyhound on the paths, Robbie began looking around for a pinch runner. I now withdrew my head, wishing I were an ostrich.

I was thinking, "If he won't use me as a pinch hitter I'm not going to stick my neck out and volunteer to be a pinch runner." Robbie, however, sighted me and called, "Tommy, how about goin' out and runnin' for Fred Heimach?"

"Uncle Robbie, I can't do it. I just can't bring myself to run for Heimach."

"What in the world's the matter with you?" Robbie said aghast. "Whatever do you mean you can't run for Heimach?"

"Robbie, a man's got some pride and he can't always swallow it and do everything somebody wants him to under those circumstances."

"What's pride got to do with it?" Robbie wanted to know.

I groaned, "Robbie, how low can you get? Here I am

going from Captain of the Phillies to pinch runner for a lefthanded pinch hitting pitcher and I just don't feel I can fall any lower than that."

Disturbed because so many of his ballplayers were hobbled by minor injuries, Uncle Robbie called a meeting and narrated a story about a certain day he was catching for the Baltimore Orioles in the first game of a doubleheader.

Robbie recalled, "In the fifth inning of the first game I caught a foul tip on the end of my little finger of my throwing hand. I looked down and the last joint was just hangin' by a little shred of flesh. I stuck the pinkie in my mouth, bit off the joint, spit it out, shoved it into the dirt and wrapped a little adhesive tape around it.

"I finished the game and also caught the second game."

Robbie had a joint missing on his little finger to vouch for the authenticity of the tale.

Then an odd thing happened. As soon as the meeting was concluded, the players began dressing for the game that afternoon and Dazzy Vance, our hottest pitcher, who was six four and weighed 230 pounds, leaned over to pull on a pair of sox, slipped, and his entire weight landed on his thumb. The thumb broke and poor Daz missed several turns.

"I guess he didn't take my talk seriously enough," Robbie said.

I'll never forget the day the color red—a vivid red—rushed into my face. We were playing at Ebbets Field and Bill Klem was umpiring behind home plate. Casey Stengel was batting and his bat was on his shoulder when Klem called him out on strikes.

Casey stayed at the plate making a pitching motion showing the pitcher's delivery and holding his hands six inches apart, then ten, and finally a foot, indicating how far the ball was outside the plate. When Casey walked away, Klem was smiling.

A few innings later I came up and Klem called me out on a third strike. I objected noisily.

"That's enough! You're through!" Klem cried, banishing me.

I wasn't going to leave until I had my say. "Sure, that's the way it is," I said resignedly. "It isn't what you say, it's who you are."

"What do you mean by that?" Klem demanded.

"I'm just a run-of-the-mill ballplayer and I get the heave-ho. But a star like Stengel stands up here, making all kinds of gestures showing how the ball was thrown and how far outside it was, and you don't run him out of the park. In fact, you even smile."

"That shows how much you know," Klem said. "Stengel was telling me about a fishing trip he was on, how he cast, and the size of the trout he caught."

The scribes really had taken a flying leap on the sobriquet "Daffy Dodgers" and "Daffiness Boys," hammering it out on their typewriters with no surcease. If the views and theories of Sigmund Freud had been accepted in this era, the public would have expected the entire team to lie down on one couch for psychoanalysis.

Admittedly they did some inexplicable things in the days during the reign of Robbie—to continue their antics under Max Carey, Casey Stengel, Burleigh Grimes, and Leo Durocher. Influenced by a gentlemanly type of manager: Burt Shotton—1949-50; Charley Dressen—1951-52-53; and Walter Alston in 1954 to the present year, there was a metamorphosis.

The Dodgers became normal.

CHAPTER 2

IT'S NO BED OF ROSES

No BASKETBALL ever bounced around more than I did after my stint as a player with the Dodgers ended in 1932. After logging fifteen years of playing time in the minors, the majors and back to the minors again, I managed Birmingham, Alabama; Hartford, Connecticut; Williamsport and Reading, Pennsylvania; Montreal; and New Orleans.

My definition of a manager is a man who the fans think has nine holes in his head large enough to be stuffed with official baseballs and can do nothing right unless he wins the pennant for his team every year.

I didn't win any pennants.

Managing a baseball team is comparable to occupying a bank teller's cage when a holdup man enters and shoves a gun into your face. If you hand over the money in the cash drawer the bank loses. Should you bravely push the alarm button you lose—your life.

Only a few persons in an entire city where you're toiling to make a creditable showing won't second-guess you —and those are the ones either too young or too old to care. Even Walt Alston, whose club just won the world championship, is not above criticism, as was exemplified during 1963 when he was leaving the stadium after losing three straight due to poor fielding.

Trying to locate his car on the parking lot, he collided with a fan.

"No offense," Walt apologized.

"You're right, Alston," the fan agreed. "And no defense either."

There are two types of managers. One is the Skipper whose entrance into the clubhouse causes all levity among the ballplayers to stop. The other is the Skipper whose entrance into the clubhouse does not disturb the normal state of affairs, and one of the men calls out, "Want to play a little cards tonight, Skipper?"

I qualified as the manager who likes cards.

I have nothing personally against the French nation. I can sing the "Marseillaise" a bit off-key, I admire the figure of Brigitte Bardot, and long may the tricolor wave. I've also heard the frequently repeated adage, "Fifty million Frenchmen can't be wrong."

This may be indisputably true. But in my opinion three Frenchmen were wrong.

The three were the trio owning the Montreal Royals baseball team in the International League: Hector Racine, Romeo Gauvreau, and Lucien Beauregard. They were tremendously successful businessmen but only a few weeks before my coming to the Canadian city had these three musketeers learned the location of first, second, and third base.

Hector Racine had an affliction: bad eyes. They were obstructed by cataracts. Watching ball games, he sat directly behind home plate, using for better vision what appeared to be a large watchmaker's eyeglass that he held over one eye. By manipulating this seeing aid, he followed the ball from pitcher to hitter and to the fielders. Sitting beside him, his partner, Romeo Gauvreau, periodically told him where to focus his attention and the glass.

On our club was a cute lefthanded veteran pitcher, Harry Smythe. He had a smooth, rapid pick-off move to first base. He would kick his foot toward first and then turn his head and throw the ball to home plate, or rotate and twist his head while looking at the batter and bullet the ball to first, trying to nip the runner.

These gyrations bothered Hector. He'd be watching Smythe when he gave a runner his best move and it appeared like he had thrown the ball toward the plate, when suddenly the runner on first was picked off. The fast, tricky motions baffled Racine, who had a terrible time adjusting his glass to keep pace.

Often as he focused on Smythe, then toward the hitter and back to the field, he would cry out exasperatedly in his thick French accent: "Romeo! Who has got the baseball?"

Racine's poor eyesight did not prevent him from second-guessing the umpires. On a crucial pitch by the opposing hurler, arbiter Chuck Solodare called it a ball. Racine, who must have had difficulty even seeing Solodare, rose in his seat and yelled, "Hey, Solodare! What ees the mattaire with you? That was a strike! The ball was on the corner!"

Each morning, regular as clockwork, Mr. Racine telephoned me to go over the previous game blow by blow. Should we be fortunate enough to have scored a victory, he magnified some ridiculous situation to astronomical proportions that in his mind caused us to win.

Such as a certain game in which Newark had men on first and second with a full count on a hit-and-run play. The batter obligingly poked a line drive to my short-stop, who tossed the ball to the second baseman and he in turn relayed the ball to first base for a rare triple play.

The following morning came my usual telephone call from Mr. Racine, who complimented: "That ees a fine play, that treeple play. We should use that play more often."

Other times he would phone, remarking, "The teams that are winning are the teams that are swinging."

Translated, this meant I had someone take a pitch in a crucial situation. I asked to what specific play he referred, and he mentioned a circumstance in the ninth inning of a game we lost in the twelfth. The bags were loaded, two out, the score tied and Luis Olmo, who later played several years for the Dodgers, was the batter.

It was a full count on Olmo. Steve Gromek was the Baltimore pitcher. He threw a side-arm change of pace curve ball to Olmo, who started to swing, checked it, decided again to hit, and finally took the three and two pitch right down the middle.

Mr. Racine wanted to know why I had Olmo take the pitch with the full count. Certainly no manager in his right mind, or even one with no mind at all, would give the batter a take sign. Yet how could I explain the workings of Olmo's mind to Mr. Racine?

The Montreal fans could be relied upon to come up with some little gem. The sacrifice they called the "scratchafice." If a visiting manager used the sacrifice and two runs crossed the plate, even though he ordered the play, hopeful of getting only one, when we batted the next inning, I, of course, couldn't call for a sacrifice, as we were too far behind.

Perhaps my hitter would hit into a double play and then the Frenchmen would yell, "Hey, Thompson, what ees the mattaire with you? Don't you like to scratchafice? She is too good for you but she work for the other fellow. He make two runs."

I had a large, muscular outfielder. Physically he appeared able to rattle the boards of any fence in the International League. Instead he was tickling the ball like his bat was made from a feather duster.

I said to him, "George, how much do you weigh?"

"Well, Skip, I weigh 230 pounds."

"Then would you mind," I said, "putting about 100 pounds of that into your next swing?"

I was sent an outfielder to replace a young fellow I had who was in too fast company. To make room for the newcomer I had to break the news that I was sending him to a lower minor league. I spoke to him like a father, trying to soften the blow, to comfort his feelings by gently pointing out his lack of experience—how he would undoubtedly gain in the long run by stepping down a notch.

"You'll probably hate me for this and spit on my grave," I concluded.

He retaliated, "You won't have to worry about that, Mr. Thompson. I don't like standing in line."

Some of the youngsters become bitter upon learning they can't stay with a team. I had one such boy who was signed as an outfielder. It was obvious after a couple of weeks that he wouldn't make much of a ballplayer. Slow on the bases, mediocre arm.

Calling him into my office, I told him we were giving him his unconditional release, explaining that baseball didn't hold much future for him and it would be squandering his time to play in the minors.

In the course of our conversation I asked, "What is your vocation?"

"Methodist," he answered.

I tried to straighten him out by explaining, "Your being a Methodist is your belief. Your vocation would be your regular trade or occupation. Like my vocation is baseball manager."

"That's your belief," he sneered.

The Dodgers had signed a mammoth pitcher, Ed Spaulding. Spaulding stood six feet five inches, weighed 225 pounds. He could throw real hard. When he was shipped to Montreal he had difficulty getting into the win column, and the front office, as well as myself, suspected that some of his extracurricular activities were causing him to lose his effectiveness.

The club hired a detective to shadow him at night. With Spaulding's huge proportions, the job seemed a cinch. The private eye handed in his first report to club officials:

> Followed suspect who met a lady with two young children. They boarded a trolley car. I did likewise. After leaving trolley they entered an apartment. Waited until morning without seeing suspect leave apartment.

It became crystal clear to club officials why Spaulding was throwing up weak pitches: this all-night partying was sapping his strength.

Later it was revealed that the bungling private detective had missed the gigantic Spaulding and followed Bob

Chipman, a slightly built pitcher who was happily married with two children and leading an exemplary life.

The club owners stopped wasting their money.

The punctuality of Mr. Racine's morning telephone calls, combined with his harping upon Luis Olmo's indecision at the plate, lit a fuse resulting in a temper explosion. Mr. Racine was the principal stockholder in a large dry goods firm, and unless the confused Olmo was thinking about merchandising, Mr. Racine couldn't possibly have understood his vacillations at the plate.

I blew my top, thundering, "Mr. Racine, I don't know anything about the dry goods business and you certainly know nothing about the baseball business. I'll leave the dry goods business alone if you'll leave the baseball business alone."

I didn't receive my customary call the next day from Mr. Racine. I did, however, get a call from the Brooklyn office. Mr. Racine had dropped a strong hint in the nature of "I think we need a new manager."

The next year I was in New Orleans, of the Southern Association. Here I spent two pleasant years. In New Orleans the sacrifice was just the plain sacrifice.

On the club we had Paul Merineau from the French section of Montreal. Paul spoke only a smattering of English. He was a better-than-average ball hawk and an excellent base runner, daring and speedy. Notwithstanding his skill in these two departments, Merineau was wielding an anemic bat.

All managers in the Dodger organization were required to send in a daily report after each game, which included the box score, a commentary, and what different players were doing or failing to do.

My report on Paul Merineau was:

> Merineau is having considerable difficulty making contact with the ball and as of now has a very low batting average. I believe that Merineau is thinking in French but the Southern Association pitchers are pitching in English.

At Birmingham in the same league I was a playing manager. To be a playing manager is the same as sticking your head in a loaded cannon. Leo Durocher was the type of playing manager who didn't seem to mind if his head *was* in the barrel of a cannon. If the cannon fired, decapitating him, somehow his head and shoulders got together again ready for the next game.

I always admired Leo's nerve. He was undoubtedly one of the finest managers I've ever been in contact with. Leo was daring, vigorous, a high-rolling gambler. He managed as he saw fit—not catering to the fans or to please writers in the press box. If he had a hunch he played it to the hilt, contradictory to all the established rules of baseball.

There was one dramatic moment in his managership that through the years remains in sharp focus. The Dodgers were facing the Cubs. It was one out in the ninth and the Dodgers had a man on third. Dolph Camilli, father of Doug, now a catcher with the Dodgers, was the hitter. Camilli was a free swinger. He led the Dodgers in home runs and runs batted in. Also strikeouts. A popular choice of the fans, he could have been elected to nearly any public office in Brooklyn. He approached the plate. But not for long. Durocher called time, walked up to Camilli and, taking the bat away from him, announced to the umpire: "Durocher for Camilli."

Removing a power hitter before 20,000 fans and sub-stituting himself was fortitude at its greatest. Boos and Bronx cheers filled the air.

Verne Olsen was the Cub pitcher. He wound up, the man on third tore for the plate, and Durocher laid down a perfect squeeze bunt. The winning run scored. Olsen, beset by rage, picked up the ball and threw it over the top deck. He then dogged Durocher all the way into the clubhouse, fuming and raging and calling him every name in the book and some banned from books sold in cities other than Boston.

Durocher was on intimate terms with a few choice expletives himself, but he smilingly checked his tongue and kept reminding Olsen, "Look at the scoreboard . . . look at the scoreboard."

The event typified Durocher. He was a sensationalist and unafraid to put himself on the spot. Had he popped up that day his body might have been discovered in the Gowanus Canal encased in concrete, with bat in hand as a reminder.

If there's an advantage for a field manager coaching at the first or third base box, it's that he can charge straight at the umpire to lodge his complaints in less time than he could from the dugout. He sprints at the ump with the speed of a downhill skier and is allowed a few minutes to blow off steam and nearly become a cardiac case.

You can't win over the boys in blue, but once I came close. It ended with a no decision verdict. At least I think it did. I never knew for sure.

In 1944 my New Orleans team was playing a game in Atlanta. Roaring like an infuriated bull, I ran from the coach's box at third over to first base umpire Jim

Tongate to criticize what I believed was his—phrasing it politely—lack of accuracy.

Finally he chased me from the game and in so doing used profanity. This was a switch. Players and managers get ejected from games for swearing at umps, but this was the only time I ever heard an umpire swear at one of us.

The next day I received a wire from league president Billy Evans—himself a former American League umpire —stating I was fined $25.00 for delaying the game and abusing the umpire. I sent him my check for the amount to cover the fine, still rankling from the curses the umpire rained upon me.

I called Mr. Evans on the telephone and asked, "Did you ever use profanity in banishing managers and players from a game?"

"Certainly not."

"Well, Jim Tongate did," I replied, listing his oaths.

"You have proof?"

"I have."

Mr. Evans promised an investigation. The season had only three days remaining and I had been home for two weeks when I received a check for $12.50—a refund of half my fine.

I never figured that one out. Was the umpire fined the other half?

People have asked me, "Did your wife play any role, vital or otherwise, in your managing?"

She certainly did.

Many nights when one of my teams was having a losing streak I, unable to sleep, would quietly creep from our bed and stand by the window, gazing into the darkness and smoking a cigaret. At such times Peg would awaken, call to me in a gentle voice, soothe me, and lead me back to bed.

Against Atlanta one of my players slid home and was called out. I thought he had beaten the throw and the tag came a fraction of a second too late. I rushed the umpire, screamed, yelled, jumped up and down. Mrs. Thompson was sitting with the players' wives behind home plate in the front row. I happened to catch her eye. She put two fingers over her mouth in a silencing gesture.

I got the message.

As I started back for the third base coaching box I said to the umpire who was ready to bounce me, "I'm not quieting down on account of you, but Mrs. Thompson has ordered me to shut up and I'll have to mind her."

There are players who don't like a manager at first sight. It can be motivated by a clash of personalities, the contour of his jaw, the sound of his voice—any one of a dozen things. Nothing can change the first opinion. I understand this. I didn't like a manager once myself. My mistake was to let him know my feelings.

He was Max Carey of the Dodgers, who followed Wilbert Robinson. The year was 1932.

We reported to the Miami Biltmore in Coral Gables, Florida, for spring training. Our exhibition schedule called for a series of games on the west coast of Florida at Clearwater, St. Petersburg, Bradenton, Sarasota. For almost a week we were away from the home training base. As custom dictates upon coming in from a trip, all of the players charged the desk for mail that may have arrived during their absence.

34

I got several letters and strolled over to a sofa (in those days it was a sofa and not a couch) with a couple of the other players. Carey picked up his mail and as he approached us he pointed to a thick stack of letters he was carrying and said, "It's a heavy mail for me, but two-thirds of it is from people asking for a job."

As he walked out of what I thought was earshot I couldn't resist remarking, "He forgot that this time last year he wrote more letters than that himself for a job."

The next day Carey proceeded to chew me out, mentioning how little he appreciated my remark. I was quite surprised that he had such sharp ears.

The following spring, the second year Carey was manager, we were coming north to engage the Jacksonville Club of the South Atlantic League in an exhibition game as Al Lopez and Ray Phelps, two of our stars, once played with that team. We were leading 8 to 3 in the first half of the eighth inning, when Carey told me to pinch hit for the pitcher.

With one out and a man on third, I hit my usual hippety-hop ground ball to the infield and was thrown out at first base with the runner unable to score. After the game in the clubhouse, Carey said, "Tommy, you missed a sign."

"Missed a sign?" I said, puzzled, as I couldn't imagine which sign I had missed in such a situation because I had hit the first pitch.

"You certainly did," he asserted.

"What sign did I miss, Max?"

"You missed the squeeze play sign."

I was surprised that a major league club would think of using a squeeze play against a Class A club when the Dodgers led by five runs in the eighth inning.

"Max," I said, "I thought the idea of the game was to fool the opposition and not your own team."

Several of my unwise expressions to Carey probably influenced a decision he was to make. When we reached Philly for our opener I smelled a mouse. Or should I say a rat? Carey seemed to be hiding from me around the hotel lobby. He'd duck behind a potted palm if I sighted him from a distance, lose himself behind a pillar or move in back of a fat man.

On the morning of our opening game John Gorman, the traveling secretary, handed me an envelope.

"Tommy, here's your ticket."

"Ticket? . . . ticket?" I repeated. "I don't need a ticket, I'm one of the players."

"You'll need *this* ticket," Gorman stated. "It's a ticket to Jersey City. They're optioning you for the season."

I made up my mind right there and then that if in the future I ever managed a baseball team and I had to fire or trade one of my boys, I'd do it personally. Carey did it the easy way for him but the hard way on a player.

A player is human. He has feelings and pride.

Waite Hoyt, the ex-Yankee pitching wizard, will back me up on this. He had been traded to the Dodgers and was having his difficulties. The Dodgers were working out on an off day with batting and infield practice. After about an hour Carey announced that he had to leave to do some radio commercials for a product called Minit-Rub, a healing salve in which he had a financial interest. Practice was turned over to Casey Stengel, one of his coaches.

Casey had them going for thirty minutes, giving Carey time to shower, dress, and leave the park, when Babe Hamberger came from the clubhouse looking for Hoyt.

Hamberger was assistant clubhouse man and general leg-man for the front office.

Finding Hoyt, he said something to him. Hoyt let out a wild cry of rage. He was practically incoherent, his face was livid.

We rushed over to find out what was the matter. At length Hoyt found his voice and we heard him say, "I pitched nineteen years in the American League and I have to come over here and get my unconditional release from a clubhouse boy. Carey didn't even have guts enough to tell me himself before he left."

When I was managing for New Orleans I had a tough bout with a heckler. In a small, intimate park catcalls and abuses hurled from the stands can trigger a temper. I had a running battle of the wisecracks lasting several years with a certain loudmouthed fan.

I first heard his strident voice—a combination of a bull elephant caught in a trap and a French horn blown off-key—the day New Orleans played at Chattanooga. It began with a reference to my home town:

"Hey, Thompson, I drove through Centerville, Alabama, the other day. That's not such a hot spot. You must be a real hayshaker, coming from there."

I swung my head around, calling back, "You live here in Chattanooga. This town certainly doesn't remind me of Paris, France. As a matter of fact, Chattanooga's the first cemetery I've ever seen with traffic lights."

A moment of silence followed and I knew my barb had struck a nerve. Then he burst into life, finding his voice with a new barrage of caustic remarks.

When World War II started the New Orleans club officials allowed enlisted military personnel to watch games free of charge, and suddenly, directly behind my defenseless back at third base, reverberated that familiar voice. I wheeled and saw an Army sergeant the size of a Sherman tank and learned he was from Camp Plauche. He was on me from opening until closing day.

"Knucklehead," "Dumbo," and "Creep" were his choice names. He was a great second-guesser. If I sent a runner in, I should have held him at third; if I held him at third, I should have sent him in; if I sacrificed with a bunt, I should have hit away; if I took the pitcher out, I should have left him in and vice versa.

I was glad when the season was over and I could rest my burning ears. I returned for a second year—something few managers did as the mortality rate was high among them here—and as I walked out to third base to coach on opening day, who should welcome me with unflattering remarks but my blimp-sized sergeant from the previous season. His voice trumpeted louder than before. He must have practiced before a photograph of me all winter.

I couldn't understand why they didn't send him overseas. He probably had some physical defect but it certainly wasn't his vocal cords. I called to him:

"Who do you know in Washington? Why aren't you in the South Pacific?"

He bellowed, "I don't see any military outfit on you, Thompson!"

Then I temporarily stopped him with, "No, Sarge, they broke the rope when they dragged you down to the draft board."

He rode my back all summer.

On the final day of the season I came to our bench and who should greet me but the sergeant. "Hey, Skipper," he requested, "how about giving me an autographed ball?"

My temper flamed. "I'll give you an autographed ball, but it will be between the eyes. Get up in the grandstand where you belong."

In Birmingham a doctor fan, one of the leading surgeons in the city, had been riding me all season. He was a season ticket holder, which, I suppose, gave him some vocal rights. My best boy was pitching a two-hitter. He had a two-run lead, but he suddenly lost his stuff, giving up a single and a walk. I decided to take him out.

As I came from the dugout this doctor, from his front row box, called, "Another mistake, Thompson?"

I turned around slowly, faced him, and said, "A mistake, Doctor? Well, at least MY mistake will be able to work tomorrow."

Players have a legitimate reason to dread rainy days. Boredom has nothing to do with it. It's purely fear. A rainy day may be the day a manager, usually having nothing else to do, picks up the phone and tries to make deals.

As a manager, I appreciated the fears of my players because of my own experience as a player. I was once attached to the Pirates during spring training at Paso Robles, California. California had seemed a sure bet to escape precipitation. Far from it. A sky is just a sky, no matter what state in the union it hangs over.

The rains came to Paso Robles. I became a one-man weather bureau, spending most of my time peering at the overcast. I even consulted an octogenarian with a rheumatic leg. I asked one of the few Indians in the city his opinion and received the answer, "I only know how to make heap big rain—not know when it stop."

Then I heard my name paged in the hotel lobby, went to the phone and the voice of Manager Bill McKechnie said, "I want to see you up in my room."

My worst fears were realized. I was sent to Kansas City and that was long before Kansas City was a major league team. The deal was necessary because the football player Indian Joe Guyon slid into Ralph Michaels, Kansas City second baseman, as if he were seeking revenge against the palefaces, and tore ligaments loose in his body.

By the time I reached the age of thirty-eight, I realized that as a manager I was on a treadmill, and always carrying a suitcase in each hand. Thirty-eight, in those days before vitamins, was a lot older than it is now. My daughter Ann was readying herself for college. My wife was becoming road-weary. Permanency was the equivalent of a word in the Hungarian language that I couldn't define because I didn't speak Hungarian. Certainly I enjoyed matching wits with other managers and working with upcoming kids trying to get them a break in the majors and feeling they were my protégés, but the challenge on the field was beginning to pale.

Attending minor league meetings in the winter, I'd sit around the hotel lobby noticing that there'd be thirty to thirty-five managers seeking jobs that didn't exist. The mortality among managers was on a par with that among spies caught out of uniform during wartime.

If you were a manager and your team was doing fine— maybe in second place—and your shortstop slid into third, breaking his leg, the team might drop into the second division. Then a hue and cry would arise and you'd be called a lousy manager. Of course the broken leg had nothing to do with it. Fans seldom pause long enough for analysis. The simple fact escapes them that when two teams play one has to lose, and there may be a good reason.

What attracted my attention at minor league meetings was the absence of front office people looking for jobs. The pressures were less on these fellows. Nobody in the front office would be called an ugly name if the team finished in last place.

I approached Branch Rickey, Jr., at one of these meetings at Jacksonville, Florida. He was Farm Director of the Dodgers under Larry MacPhail. I told him I wanted front office work. He handed me a job at $450 per month in the minor league department. That first winter I took World Series films and went around exhibiting them to high schools, churches, and clubs, besides planning spring training for the following year.

Then before I knew what happened I was back managing again.

The Dodgers bought a ball club—Reading, Pennsylvania—from a chicken farmer named Robert Addington. I was sent down to watch them play and tender any advice I could give to the home office.

The chicken farm owner was depressed, mainly because when the team lost some of the fans threw eggs. Trying to cheer him up, I said, "The club really isn't that bad."

"That's not what's bothering me."

Puzzled, I waited and heard him say, "If they want to throw eggs at my players they could at least throw my own brand."

Addington was losing a little money and decided he

belonged back on the farm where a chicken didn't have to know how to hit, field, or pitch—only how to lay an egg.

In 1941 the Dodgers took over active operation of the Reading club, with me as its Field Manager.

The club owned a reasonably new Chevrolet bus, forty uniforms—home and road—and fifteen players, one of whom was Carl Furillo, later to become an all-time Dodger great in the field. However, at this time Furillo was a long way from the outfield. He was a pitcher. He could throw real hard. In the first game I started him, he broke a player's wrist and in his next appearance a couple of ribs. I told Carl that I was going to have to find another position for him. I was fearful—due to the small rosters of the clubs—that there'd be a general man-power shortage around the league if Furillo was allowed to continue pitching. So I shifted him to the outfield.

Lee MacPhail, Larry's son, just out of Swarthmore College, came down to begin his career in professional baseball as our club's Business Manager. The following year I was back at my regular duties visiting spring training camps from Durham, North Carolina, to Wilson in the same state, and on to Staunton, Virginia.

Then it happened again!

The week before season's opener the manager of the Johnstown, Pennsylvania, club of the Pennsylvania State Association was drafted into military service. Larry Mac-Phail ordered me to Johnstown to manage the club until a replacement could be found. It would, MacPhail promised, last only a few weeks.

The weeks ran into more weeks. The temporary job was fast becoming permanent. The managerial harness was tightening. I had left my wife in New York and might as well have been a bachelor again. Just before Decoration Day I telephoned MacPhail. For once I outtalked him, but only because I hung up before he could think of an answer:

"Larry, if you don't get a manager down here within three days I'm going to put all the players' names in a hat and draw one out and whoever the lucky or unlucky one is, I'm going to say, 'You're the new manager.' "

A replacement arrived.

CHAPTER 3

A POCKETFUL OF SCHEMES

LELAND STANFORD MACPHAIL was a name to remember. In 1938 he became Executive Vice-President of the Dodgers. A brilliant scholar in his undergraduate days, he had been an athlete, a lawyer, a merchant, a banker, a baseball operator, and, as a soldier in World War I, hatched a plot to kidnap the Kaiser that barely missed success. Had it succeeded intimates of MacPhail were certain that the blatant Scotsman would have profited handsomely by exhibiting Europe's hated man on the road.

He was an outstanding promoter, schemer, strategist. He could have instigated a love battle between Tristan and Isolde, or ironed out the hereditary difficulties between a strange dog and cat. Brusque and brash, MacPhail, before he bade farewell to baseball, parlayed raw nerve, a glib tongue, business acumen, and initiative into a million dollars after taxes. His reign was an autocratic one, but it augured well for the slipping Dodgers.

Shrewd and farsighted, MacPhail was constantly dreaming up gimmicks to increase the gate. Some of them paid off. His installation of lights in Ebbets Field for night baseball was a real shot in the arm to attendance. Innovation followed innovation. New faces made weekly appearances on the field. He came up with an electric organ and hired a Miss Gladys Gooding to send out tunes on it. All went smoothly until the versatile Miss Gooding played "Three Blind Mice" as the umps marched from their dressing room to home plate. It was a toss-up whether the suggestion came from MacPhail or Durocher.

MacPhail had a temper that needed little prodding to break the leashes of self-control. A constant source of his irascibility was triggered either consciously or unconsciously by his field manager, Leo Durocher, who had succeeded Burleigh Grimes. MacPhail fired and rehired him on the average of every two weeks. Leo was his whipping boy, but Leo was unscarred from the lashings. With Leo on the field and MacPhail behind the scenes there were constant fireworks. No one had to wait until the Fourth of July for pyrotechnics.

Three years after MacPhail and Durocher combined their talents the Dodgers were playing the Yankees in the World Series.

The Dodgers were in shaky financial shape when MacPhail moved in. Their bank balance was striking out. They were controlled and largely owned by the Brooklyn Trust Company. The team—down in the standings—failed to lure customers and the mere click of a turnstile could be heard as far away as Empire Boulevard. Their nickname of "Bums" was at this time very appropriate. It could have referred to any checks the organization cashed.

The team owed the bank close to $800,000. MacPhail called a conference. His bubbling optimism was infectious. He explained that there wasn't a chance of paying off any of the principal, but if he could have an additional loan to buy some players, he firmly believed he could pull the club out of hock.

His persuasiveness melted the ice in the bankers' veins and filled their hearts with expectation. The word castles he had built in the smoky air seemed so impregnable that he was able to talk them out of $350,000. An immediate purchase was Joe Medwick, followed by Dolph Camilli and the signing of a flock of "free agents."

In 1941 when the Dodgers won the first pennant they had captured since 1920, the drought was ended.

Among MacPhail's multiplicity of troubles were umpires and adjusting to life in general. Umpires were ogres to him, walking demons sent up from the fetid pits of hell to plague and oppress him personally. If anyone had waved the blue coat of an umpire in front of MacPhail, his reaction would have been like a bull's upon seeing red.

There was the day when MacPhail was sitting with Buzzie Bavasi and me when a close play occurred at home plate. An opposing player slid in and when the cloud of dust vanished the umpire signaled him safe.

"That guy was out!" MacPhail bellowed.

"I thought he was safe," Bavasi said softly.

A stream of curses flowed from MacPhail, during which Buzzie was fired for *his* first time. Later on the same day he was up in the press box and here accosted Bill Klem, an ex-ump himself, who was then acting as supervisor of his National League colleagues. MacPhail began rehashing the play. He started berating Klem as an umpire, expanding the discussion to belittle every umpire working under him.

A two-man war exploded. MacPhail threw his strongest ammunition—expletives—into the raging combat. Klem never employed profanities. He had a special name, however, stored for just such an occasion. Turning toward the red-faced MacPhail, he released it:

"Sir, you are an apple head."

Turning the color of the fruit he was accused of resembling, MacPhail countered with a threat to punch Klem in the nose.

"Sir," Klem said coolly, "you do not frighten me. You get your courage out of a bottle."

MacPhail sputtered and walked from the press box. The soft words spoken by Klem had hardened into a formidable defense for his boys in blue.

Buzzie Bavasi then, as now, was one of the top men in his trade. Choosing the current Bavasi as the subject of his column, Arthur Daley, veteran *New York Times* sportswriter, said:

> It isn't often that ballplayers rave about a front-office figure, but they are nuts about Buzzie. They even sign blank contracts, knowing that he'll be more than fair in filling in salary figures even above expectations. He is their confidant, counselor, and friend. Just before the crucial Cardinal series, some Dodger offered an idea to his mates.
>
> "Let's win this for Buzzie," he said. And they did.
>
> But the character of the man was best illustrated, perhaps, when he invited a retired Brooklyn baseball writer, Roscoe McGowen, to be his guest at all World Series games as a member of the official party. This was a generous gesture even above and beyond the call of duty.

Recently Bavasi had trouble with one of his star performers coming to terms at contract time. The crux of the matter was that this player just wanted to be sure that he was going to get a larger salary than his roommate. Buzzie invited the player to drop into his office.

Prior to the player's appearance Buzzie instructed his secretary to prepare a contract for his roommate. Into this contract he had inserted figures calling for about $2,000 less than his roommate was actually being paid. Buzzie laid the contract on his desk, conspicuously exposed.

Buzzie had previously arranged for his secretary to call him away from the office after he and the player had been in conference for ten minutes. She stepped in and said, "Pardon me, Mr. Bavasi, Mr. O'Malley would like to see you in his office."

Buzzie excused himself and walked out, knowing full well that the player's curiosity would be aroused and he would sneak a peek at the contract.

When he returned and again began negotiations, Buzzie was able to sign this player for $1,000 more than the figure contained in the contract on the desk. The player was delighted to know he was being offered more than he thought his roommate was to receive.

Buzzie is fair-minded and it isn't necessary for him to resort to trickery or subterfuges, with the exception of this case I cited where the ego of a man made unfair demands. On the modern Dodgers, the holdouts are fewer than with most teams, there having been no serious ones in the last decade. Nearly every spring we go into training with all our players signed.

The Dodgers under Rickey signed a fine young pitcher, Billy Loes. He had been outstanding as a high-school flinger around the metropolitan area. He was assigned to pitch against the Cards at the period when Stan Musial was at the pinnacle of his career and had a special fondness for Ebbets Field, hitting nearly .400 there.

Loes decided to consult with Carl Erskine, one of the vets on the club, asking him, "What's the best way to pitch to Musial?"

"I'm glad you asked me that," Erskine replied knowingly. "I've had pretty good success with Stan."

Loes was all ears. "How?" he asked.

"By throwing him my best pitch and backing up third."

Billy developed fast. He could boast of a tremendous arm and he knew the weaknesses of scores of National League hitters. His second year he won 10 and lost 4. For this Buzzie gave him his first really good contract— $15,000 per year.

After signing Billy, Buzzie counseled, "I think you should take out some insurance."

Billy showed surprise. "Why should I take out insurance?"

"Because," Bavasi explained, "you're making real good money now, your mother and father aren't too well, and your father is unable to work because of a physical handicap. It would be a nice gesture if you took out an insurance policy providing for them in the event anything happened to you."

Much to Buzzie's amazement, Billy said, "Me take out insurance! Why, for goodness' sakes, if anything ever happened to me my mother and father would kill themselves."

Before Buzzie could answer, Billy continued: "What good would any insurance policy do them then? Probably go to some undeserving relative."

49

The Dodgers used to play a couple of exhibition games with the Yankees prior to opening the season. One of the pleasures derived from this game was visiting with their pitcher, Lefty Gomez. He was as capable a raconteur as he was a hurler. Here's a story he told us:

"I'll never forget one of my earliest experiences with the Yankees. I was in the bullpen and had never been in a major league game. Herb Pennock was leading 2 to 1 in the eighth and a hard liner comes tearing right at him and knocks him down.

"So they called me. A lot of things run through your head when you're going in to relieve in a troubled spot. One of them was, 'Should I spike myself.' When I got up there Joe McCarthy was waiting.

" 'Okay, Boss,' I told him, 'I know what the situation is. This is the way I'll pitch to him.' And I outlined my strategy against big Jim Foxx of the Athletics.

"McCarthy looked at me and said, 'What's the matter with you, Gomez? That line drive broke the webbing in Pennock's glove. All I want you to do is give him your glove and go back and sit down on the bench.' "

For every story Gomez could rattle off, someone was able to retaliate by telling one on him. The one appealing to me most involved Yankee third base coach Art Fletcher, former Giant shortstop under John McGraw.

Gomez, as everyone was well aware, was a very poor hitter. Came one game when he finally reached third. While he was there, Lefty noticed that the pitcher was taking a long, careless windup, apparently ignoring him.

He swung his head in Fletcher's direction and said, "Art, I think I can steal home on this guy."

"Gomez," Fletcher bristled, "it took you ten years to

get to third base and now you want to louse it up. Stay there."

MacPhail's 1940 Dodgers finished second and the boss of the Bums began sniffing the sweet smell of the pennant. He believed that with a catcher and another pitcher his team might go all the way. He wanted catcher Mickey Owens from the Cards and pitcher Kirby Higbe from the Phillies. With his usual farsightedness, MacPhail knew that Branch Rickey of the Cardinals wouldn't strengthen the Dodgers' catching if he suspected that they were successful in their efforts to secure a front line pitcher.

In early November MacPhail closed a deal with the Phillies on Higbe for a reported $100,000. He insisted that the Phils hold off any announcement of the transaction until he had Owens in the fold. Rickey consented to selling Owens to make room on the Cards for Walker Cooper, a fine young catching prospect in the farm organization.

I'm certain that if Rickey had gotten wind MacPhail had already acquired Higbe, Owens would have wound up with some club other than the Dodgers. These two players, with the later addition of second baseman Billy Herman, brought the Dodger faithful their first pennant in twenty-one years.

This was the year the Brooklyn and New York sportswriters at their annual winter baseball dinner and show dedicated a song to Larry MacPhail titled: I'VE GOT A POCKETFUL OF SCHEMES.

Under MacPhail's five year leadership the Dodgers averaged over a million spectators each season. A club that had been a chronic second division finisher and struggling

51

to free itself of indebtedness to the bank now became one of the choice franchises in the league.

After winning the pennant in 1941, they lost the 1942 bunting to a remarkably strong Cardinal team, notwithstanding the fact that the Dodgers at one time during the race held a 10½ game lead. They won 104 games—customarily good enough for a pennant. Instead of exuding confidence when the Dodgers were enjoying their substantial lead, MacPhail made a prophetic statement. He categorically declared they would lose the championship; and he bitterly assailed Manager Durocher and his mates, accusing them of becoming fat, slovenly, showing no hustle, expecting the other teams to roll over and play dead.

The Cards won the pennant by four games.

During August and September the Dodgers were bobbing in and falling out of first place with the regularity of a bird in a cuckoo clock. This was when a story circulated in Brooklyn. A rabid fan, unable to take it any more, seemed headed for a nervous crackup. He couldn't eat, couldn't sleep. He went to a doctor, unburdened his troubles.

"Doc, I get in bed and I find myself pitching for Hugh Casey, playing shortstop for PeeWee Reese, chasing flies in center field for Pete Reiser."

The doctor nodded sagely, agreeing this would mentally disturb anyone, and suggested the fan get another interest. He advised his patient that the next time he felt an attack like this coming on, just to close his eyes and imagine he was dancing with a beautiful (38-26-36) blonde with eyes of blue, to the melodic strains of Guy Lombardo's orchestra.

The fan, staring wide-eyed at the doctor, exclaimed, "What! and miss my turn at bat?!"

MacPhail had a robust sense of humor. If something amused him he wanted to share it with others. In the late winter I was sitting at my desk when the buzzer from his office rang and he asked me to step in. Grinning from ear to ear, he related that he was having contractual difficulties with Higbe. Higbe had just finished a pretty good season. He wanted more money from MacPhail.

Handing me a letter he had just received from his pitcher, he said, "I think you'll get a kick out of this."

Dear Larry:

Received your contract and of course it's impossible for me to sign at those terms. My father-in-law has been after me for several years to go into business with him. He operates a chain of drugstores throughout South Carolina and my wife is concerned about my traveling so much. I think that if this is your best offer I'll have to seriously consider going in the drug business with my father-in-law. Sorry.

Kirby

P.S. Please send me a thousand advance on next year's salary.

I had worked a number of weeks for MacPhail and had still not received my first salary check. I consulted Bavasi. Buzzie related that he labored seven weeks for MacPhail before he was put on the payroll.

"I've broken your record by three weeks, and Christmas **is** coming," I complained.

Cornering MacPhail, I made clear my plight. "I'm sorry," he apologized. "We just haven't had a meeting of the Board of Directors to set your salary."

MacPhail, I suppose, wished to make me feel good because I knew a meeting of the Board of Directors wasn't necessary to decide my nominal salary, the amount of which had already been discussed.

"Go see the auditor and tell him to give you an advance of a hundred dollars," he instructed.

After explaining how long I'd worked for the organization, he said, "Gee, Fresco, I had no idea the length of time you've been with us. You go and tell Bill Gibson to let you have whatever you need."

I drew $200. My first Dodger paycheck since my managerial days.

MacPhail was never one to assume blame for any mistakes. In 1942 when Branch Rickey, Jr., and I were operating what we called Class B camp at Durham, North Carolina, MacPhail stopped off to confer with us on his return to Brooklyn from Florida.

We had about fifty players working out on various parts of the ball field. They covered nearly every blade of grass. The three of us were sitting in the stands watching practice when MacPhail asked, "Who's that fat kid limping around the infield?"

We informed MacPhail that he was a young infielder who had played at Newport, Arkansas, in the Northeast Arkansas League. During three years of operating the Newport team he was the only player batting .300. We also added that the average cellar was better lighted than the Newport Park. Fans along the sidelines drove cars up to the open field, leaving their headlights on so they could follow the ball.

MacPhail was unconvinced, insisting, "He's too fat and he must have a bad leg. I'm tired feeding these kids who aren't going anywhere. Release him."

Pleading failed to change his mind. He was adamant. We drove the boy over to Edenton, North Carolina, where the Lancaster, Pennsylvania, team, an affiliate of the Athletics, trained. They were short of players and were happy to try out anybody we released.

The infielder hit .396 for the Class B Lancaster club and was sold to the Athletics at the end of the season. He was George Kell, who played sixteen years in the American League, winding up with a .306 batting average and making the league all-star team ten times.

MacPhail had a fast reply when a sportswriter asked how Kell had managed to slip from his grasp:

Branch, Jr., and Fresco Thompson pulled a boner on that one."

In the late summer of 1942 I was in MacPhail's office when he startled me by announcing that he was going into the Army. I said, "Mr. MacPhail, you're over fifty years of age. You don't have to enter military service," and I thought of saying, but didn't, "Aren't you getting enough fighting in this country with Leo Durocher?"

"Oh, yes I do," he answered. "I'm deeply in debt and if I go into the Army I'll have a chance to catch my breath."

He pointed out that those in military service were granted a moratorium on all financial obligations until discharged.

Before MacPhail's decision, stories had been written to the effect that despite the tremendous success of the Dodgers the pressure was being applied from Dodger stockholders for him to resign. It was reported that even though he was making the money that eventually was to put the club in the black with the Brooklyn Trust Company, the owners were unhappy over some of his deals and his plowing back some of the profits into the farm system.

Sixty thousand dollars for Buck Newsome was a bone

of contention because the pitcher failed to reach his potential. Stockholders and directors forgot Dolph Camilli, a steal for $75,000, PeeWee Reese for $50,000, and it was grand larceny obtaining Pete Reiser for $100 in addition to a flock of fringe minor league players.

I wish to set the record straight by stating that Larry MacPhail was not asked to resign from the Dodgers.

He had made excellent money, but he lived high and traveled first class. I knew it was inevitable that while MacPhail (who was to be commissioned a major) was in the Army, this alert, imaginative man would figure out some project to eliminate his debts even if it meant stopping a Nazi bullet.

True enough, he formed a syndicate to purchase the New York Yankees. Three years later he retired a millionaire, to breed horses and live a life of ease as a gentleman farmer on the eastern shore of Maryland.

Before his departure to wear the uniform of Uncle Sam, the Dodger players (and MacPhail had had trouble with practically every one of them) requested his presence in the clubhouse where Captain Dolph Camilli, acting for his teammates, presented him with an expensive wrist watch.

MacPhail, temporarily stripped of his fire-eater veneer, broke down and cried.

When he returned from the service and assumed his Yankee duties, he felt an obligation toward Bavasi and me, offering us both jobs. We had both spent the majority of our careers in the National League and decided to stay with the Dodgers, a decision we never regretted.

56

CHAPTER 4

HAIL TO BRANCH RICKEY!

WHEN Larry MacPhail was being fitted for his Army uniform, directors of the Dodgers began casting around for a new general manager. Branch Rickey, Jr., had read his father was a candidate, and the printed words, vague as they were, brought a moisture to his eyes. The droplets of saline fluid were not induced by sentimentality. On the contrary, they were caused by a vexation of spirit.

He fervently hoped his parent—a noted pundit of baseball—wouldn't consider the move. Emulating his father, the younger Rickey had developed a fine farm system that was beginning to compete with the Cardinals.

Over a cup of coffee, Branch, Jr., poured out his troubled mind to me. "Larry MacPhail gave me a responsibility and certain liberties that I know I won't have under my father. I have an identity here. When the old man arrives I'll just go back to being a junior again."

The Rickeys had been referred to as the Branch and the Twig. The younger Rickey resented this. "Twigs break," he grumbled.

Branch Rickey did come to the Dodgers from St. Louis along with a flock of subordinates, many of whom were "yes men." Occasionally Bavasi and I would startle the new boss, as we were the only ones in the organization whose heads moved sideways.

"Those two must have palsy," Rickey was heard to mutter, as he wasn't used to anyone disagreeing with him.

It is difficult to describe Wesley Branch Rickey, age sixty-one, when he first became enthroned in Brooklyn to occupy a position of sovereign power and dignity. He reminded me of a Chautauqua lecturer always on stage. He was a calculating man, an astute student of the game, its complexities and tangents.

Dr. Eliot could never have crammed the voluminous history of Branch Rickey into his famed "five foot shelf." It would have necessitated carpenters enlarging the shelves up to 100 feet to accommodate the saga of this man.

If the machinations of Rickey's mind had been observed through a super-powered fluoroscope showing the brain cells arriving at conclusions by serpentine excursions into labyrinthine passages, medical science might be amazed.

The most concise writer in the world wasn't capable of furnishing a thumbnail description of Rickey. By the same token, if Rickey were requested to pen a capsule characterization of one of his players, it could amount to a trilogy.

Rickey and Casey Stengel share one thing in common: they are the only living men who can speak a foreign language in English, to leave listeners in a state of despair and utter confusion.

Four times during our association I asked Rickey for a

raise in salary, and four times I staggered from his office bewildered, befuddled, bemused by his rhetorical skill. I got no raise but I got four changes in titles.

None of us had the nerve to call Rickey cheap—unless it was some departing player traded away. If we ever made a crack at his parsimony, it was heavily veiled or we used double entendre so we had a hasty exit to travel if he took affront.

During the War, at an office meeting, Rickey was bemoaning the fact that it was impossible to buy a new automobile as the plants had shut down.

"I'd like to get a new Ford," he said longingly.

I piped up, "I'd like to get a Cadillac."

Rickey was shocked, asked, "How can you afford a Cadillac on your salary?"

"Mr. Rickey, if I have to get along without a car, I'd rather get along without a Cadillac than a Ford," I told him.

Rickey was a master of minuscule details. Suppose, for instance, a stranger in a city asked how to reach a certain address. The concise answer might be: "Go west four blocks, ..."

Should Rickey be giving directions, he would be apt to say, "Proceed in a westerly direction (listing every store passed en route for four blocks) take a sharp right turn at a ninety degree angle, walk 550 feet until you see a traffic policeman with light blue eyes and standing five feet eleven and three-quarter inches tall. Ask him."

Rickey was a devout Abraham Lincoln buff, although his personal practices were at cross-purposes with those of the Great Emancipator. Lincoln, according to history, freed the slaves. Rickey, according to baseball history, held them in bondage on low salaries. Whether it was better to stoop and pick cotton all day or leap to catch a ball was a moot question. The pay was about equal.

Rickey, a teetotaler, frowned upon the drinking of alcoholic beverages. If a doctor had told him to take a jigger for medicinal purposes he would have changed doctors. MacPhail was just the opposite. Had he found a physician who believed that liquor was the elixir of life, the chances are that MacPhail might have become his patient.

Shortly after Rickey's arrival in Brooklyn, John McDonald, the traveling secretary of the club, and I were cleaning out MacPhail's desk, when McDonald unearthed a bottle of Canadian Club whiskey. Rickey stared horrified at the bottle. McDonald, covering up for the absent owner, explained that MacPhail worked long hours in the office and kept a bottle of whiskey around purely as a health tonic. Mr. Rickey carted the bottle away and I suspect poured the contents down the drain.

A few weeks passed, and Rickey began formulating plans for the 1943 season. He called McDonald in to discuss his future and in the course of the conversation mentioned, "John, how would you like to have the Canadian club?"

Remembering the bottle of whiskey he found in MacPhail's desk, and not realizing Rickey was referring to the Montreal baseball team, McDonald answered, "Well, Mr. Rickey, if you're not going to use it, I'd be very happy to have it."

Some people wait a lifetime for an inheritance. Rickey received one before the ink was dry on his contract as major-domo of Brooklyn: Leo Durocher. They were well acquainted. It was while earlier in his career in St. Louis that Leo plunged into financial hot water and came up gasping. Rickey made Leo his reclamation project. He handled Leo's finances, paid off his bills. He admired Leo's daring and gambling instincts on the field, if not his gambling instincts off the field.

Soon after Rickey arrived in Brooklyn, Leo received a letter. It was a notice to report to his draft board for a physical. I noted a glint of hope in the eyes of Rickey and son that Uncle Sam was going to solve their dilemma; I strongly suspected they wanted to unload Leo.

Branch, Jr., accompanied Leo to his physical. He must have gone as a bird dog for his father. I can think of no other valid reason. Leo was perfectly capable of dressing and undressing himself without help. When Branch, Jr., came back he appeared sad.

"What was the verdict?" I asked.

"Classified 4-F because of a punctured eardrum," he said morosely.

Leo's chewing out of players and umpires had probably punctured many an eardrum during his years in baseball, but how his own got into this condition caused a wag to remark, "His voice must have boomeranged off the fence."

One of the more serious problems that Rickey had to contend with as head of the Dodgers was a clubhouse rhubarb in 1943 that threatened widespread repercussions. Leo and Buck Newsome became embroiled over the choice of a pitch to an opposing batsman in a key situation. Both argued vociferously. Newsome lost. He was suspended.

The next day, third baseman Arky Vaughn, a taciturn fellow who only said "Hello" in the spring and "Goodbye" in the fall, walked into Leo's office, handed him his uniform and made no bones about what he wanted Leo to do with it.

Joining forces with Vaughn in the battle was Dixie Walker, who strenuously objected to the treatment of Newsome. The hassle reached Rickey and he acted as peacemaker. Shortly thereafter Newsome was traded to the St. Louis Browns and gossip had it that Leo would have liked to include Vaughn and Walker among the departures but that Rickey couldn't make a satisfactory deal for them.

Rickey was a stickler for punctuality and on his frequent plane jaunts to visit various farm clubs at Fort Worth, St. Paul, Mobile, etc., he never waited for late-arriving members of his party. One spring, Rickey, his wife, Jane Moulton Rickey, and a grandchild were going to fly from Vero Beach to Fort Worth. Six A.M. was the scheduled departure. Rickey was at the airport shortly before flight time, but there was no sign of his wife or grandson.

He made a concession of two minutes, then called to the pilot, "Let's go!"

Five minutes later Mrs. Rickey and grandson reached the airport and asked Bavasi where her husband was. Pointing to a fast-vanishing speck in the sky, Bavasi said, "There he goes."

Mrs. Rickey, slightly irked, said to Bavasi, "Is there any way that we can contact Mr. Rickey?—and if so will you please tell him to keep going. He's headed in the right direction."

Bavasi shrugged. "The only way I know is through God, and Mr. Rickey may not want to speak with him."

On trips when club officials were flying with Rickey,

we might be holding a conversation and right in the middle of a sentence he would say, "Boys, I'm tired. I think I'll take a little nap. Give me twenty-five minutes."

It was mandatory to awaken him at the prescribed time. He would blink a couple of times and resume in the middle of the very sentence he last uttered before he fell asleep.

It was not unusual for Rickey to push a buzzer summoning me into his office around 10:00 A.M. when the Dodgers were playing in Philadelphia, and ask me to accompany him to that city. On one of these typical last minute rushes we hopped into a cab, boarding the train at Pennsylvania Station just before it started away.

We were pulling into Trenton when the Dodger boss clapped his hands together, exclaiming, "Oh, my God! I was supposed to meet Jane at the information window back in New York."

To paraphrase the lyrics of an old song . . ."Somewhere, someone is waiting," and to it could be added, "For Branch Rickey, nearly all the time." Often it was Jane.

I discovered that Rickey disliked jokes at his own expense. In a Fort Worth dining room Rickey, his wife, his secretary, Jane Ann Jones, and I were breakfasting. Rickey ordered tomato juice, which trickled from chin to shirt; medium boiled eggs splattered on his shirt; coffee also decorated the front of it.

At the conclusion of the meal Rickey began looking around the dining room. "Can I help you, Mr. Rickey?" I volunteered.

He shook his head. "I just want the waitress to bring the check."

I retorted, "Mr. Rickey, you don't need a check. Just

63

show the cashier your shirt and she can figure out the bill."

He did not laugh.

While Rickey was forgetful, he was never thoughtless. If he made a promise he tried to live up to it, despite the handicap of too many things on his mind. One of the promises he fulfilled was made to Edgar Allen, Mobile club owner. Rickey told Allen he would attend the opening game of the Southern Association in Mobile.

We were training in Pensacola, Florida, and Wally Dashiell, a former ballplayer who was active in civic affairs in Pensacola, had agreed to drive Rickey, myself and coaches George Sisler and Andy High to see the game.

Wally and the rest of us waited around and Rickey didn't show. At last he came in wearing a sport shirt, khaki pants, and a white duck hat. His pants were salt-water-soaked. He had been on a fishing trip and his appearance lent belief that somewhere in the warm waters off the Florida Coast was a happy fish who had won a battle to go free.

We realized that if Rickey took a shower and changed clothes we'd never make it in time to Mobile. Those were not his intentions.

"Let's go," he said, "I'm ready," and we piled in Wally's car.

Six miles from Pensacola Rickey inquired, "Do you have a heater in this car?"

"Certainly," Dashiell replied, "but I don't think you really need it, Mr. Rickey, it's a nice, balmy . . ."

"Turn it on," Rickey said.

"But . . ."

64

"I see you have one for the back and one for the front. Just turn on the back one, please," he insisted.

Dashiell shrugged and snapped on the heater switch. Hot air flooded the back portion of the car. I became curious, wondering why, on such a fine night, my boss wanted heat. I twisted around in the seat to steal a glance at him. He was down on the car floor, his posterior pushed close to the heater drying his wet pants.

We arrived at the ball park as the game started. Rickey appeared a candidate for the list of the ten worst-dressed men in the United States, bearing no resemblance to what fans might have pictured the President of the Brooklyn Dodgers to be.

If any of our players had seen him it was likely they might have voluntarily asked for a cut in salary. And this would have pleased him very much.

In spring training Rickey hated to gaze at a ball field flooded with sunshine and not see players dotting the diamond. And because the sun is fairly omnipresent in Florida, we were on the field from 9:00 A.M. until 4:00 P.M.

One day, when the Chamber of Commerce was double-crossed, there was a downpour and we huddled for protection in a little shack used by pitchers for changing shirts after batting practice workouts. After a forty-five minute deluge slackened, I inspected the field. It oozed mud. A sensible alligator would have thought twice before crossing it.

Rather than risk injury under the slippery conditions, I dismissed the players. They drove back to their barracks, passing Rickey on his way to the field. Just before he stepped from his car the sun blazed forth, the clouds drifted away, and it became crystal clear. There was, however, still thunder in the air, but it now was concentrated in Rickey's voice.

"Who called off the workout?" he roared.

"I did," I answered meekly.

"Look at that beautiful sky!"

I did, and said, "I know, Mr. Rickey, but they're not playing up there. We have to play down here in the mud."

"Get hold of your managers, round up those teams, and bring them back," he ordered.

I raced to obey. Most of the players were in the barracks, but one had already escaped to a beer tavern and I snagged him in the middle of the first bottle. When all the players and managers were corralled and we returned to the field, one of them pointed out a window of the bus and yelled, "I can't believe it!"

There was Rickey around the shortstop position, his shoes and sox off, trousers rolled up to his knees. He reminded me of a clam digger. He carried a brush, a rake, and a shovel, and was attempting to push water off the infield into the outfield. He was determined to have a ball game and that was the last time I ever called off a practice session as long as you could see the infielders' heads above water.

While we were at Vero Beach we had an incident with the police, precipitated by Don Newcombe and a member of the Washington Senators, Mike Guerra. Guerra was a white man who had managed a team in the Cuban Winter League where Newcombe played for him. Differences in opinion led to Newcombe's suspension.

When the Washington club came over to play us, Newcombe and Guerra repeated their argument from the previous season. A local sheriff sitting in the stands blew up the affair to the proportions of a race riot, arresting— of course—Newcombe. We were finally able to free him.

Rickey was concerned. He suggested to Bavasi that the next morning he round up all our Negro players—numbering a dozen out of the 500 we had in camp—and bring them to his cottage.

"What time, Mr. Rickey?" Bavasi asked.

"Five A.M."

At 4:30 Bavasi was knocking on doors and at the appointed hour was shepherding his flock to Rickey's quarters. Rickey delivered a speech, dwelling on the facts of life below the Mason-Dixon Line, how the Dodgers had no voice in the established segregation laws, and concluding with an appeal: "When in Rome, do as the Romans do or it might constitute a serious setback to your people in other fields of endeavor."

Roy Campanella, a philosopher and the most popular Negro player in the majors, turned to Newcombe. "Don," he said, "if you wants to go back to New Jersey and run an elevator, that's your business—but old Campy likes it here. I'm goin' along with the way the people of the South wants us to do."

No camaraderie existed between Rickey and his hirelings. He seldom fraternized with them, his attitude duplicating that of Paul Brown, former coach of the Cleveland Browns football team. Yet he held their respect. A humorous illustration of this occurred when Bobby Bragan was managing Fort Worth in the Texas League. Rickey sent him a lengthy telegram telling him he was thinking of bringing up Carl Erskine, the pitcher, from

Bragan's team and asked if he could help the Dodgers most as a starter or a reliefer.

Bragan wired back a terse "Yes."

Rickey wired: "Yes what?"

Bragan wired: "Yes, sir."

Rookies were still what the name implied in those days and never a member of the fraternity of veterans. The established players, realizing that these ambitious kids were some day going to latch on to their jobs, made it tough as possible on them throughout spring training.

When the rookies walked to the home plate, picked up a bat for practice, one of the vets would bark, "What the hell you doin' up here? You come out at 8:00 o'clock in the morning if you want to hit." The maltreated rookies would leave the hotel at about 7:30 A.M. and pitch to each other.

They made it miserable for the fledglings with more forms of hazing than old-fashioned college movies. A favorite trick was to ask a rookie if he was using the hotel elevator. If he said "yes," that he had a room on the fourth floor, they warned him just to wait until he received his bill: the management charged five cents per floor whenever he rode up to his room. Some of the kids would then walk up all during spring training.

Then things changed quickly. Educated players crowded team rosters. Sophomoric conduct vanished. An era of compassion and sportsmanship developed. Gil Hodges, PeeWee Reese, and Roy Campanella, to name just a few on one team, would work with the rookies, advising, coaching. Today, a pitcher like Sandy Koufax devotes hours of his time teaching rookies how to throw curves, change of pace, the moves toward first base.

Once a player stepped into the arena of salary debate

with Rickey, he had less chance of winning than a girls' softball team against the National League All-Stars. Rickey struck a hard bargain. When he was associated with the Cardinals he had Marty Marion who became known as "Mr. Shortstop." Rickey and Marion were having contractual difficulties and wiring each other back and forth.

Rickey wired: "Accept terms I have offered and I'll take care of you."

Marion's return wire said: "Give me what I want and I'll take care of myself."

Billy Loes and Rickey were arguing over contracts. Rickey didn't see eye to eye on the figure Billy wanted. At length they came to terms and Rickey, wishing to make a public announcement and get some space in the newspapers, said, "Now, Billy, I'd appreciate it if you'd keep the terms of this contract secret."

Billy quipped, "Don't worry, I'm just as ashamed of the figures as you are."

Several famous sports columnists rode Rickey hard for his penurious tactics. "Cheapo" was one of the more innocuous words showered upon him. Yet Rickey had bursts of sudden generosity that were unfathomable. For instance, at the end of the 1946 season—not a pennant-winning one—he gave every member of the Dodger varsity a new car. Today it's considered a gargantuan event when *Sport Magazine* annually awards a car to a single outstanding player.

Buzzie Bavasi cost Rickey a little money at one time. No cries of distress or even low whines came from Rickey, but not being a mind reader I couldn't tell if he suffered to any extent.

A young left-handed pitcher named Roy Sanner of

69

Arkinda, Arkansas, reported to the Dodgers while they were training at Bear Mountain, New York, during the War. It was the dead of winter and Roy checked in wearing thin summer slacks and a lightweight jacket, the sleeves of which were several inches too short. He was also hatless.

Rickey saw the kid on the ball field and in the West Point Field House where we worked out in bad weather. He instructed Buzzie to take him to New York and outfit him properly before he froze to death. Right here is where Rickey made a costly mistake. Buzzie was a fashion plate and when he went on a shopping spree, prices were unimportant.

He took Sanner to De Pinna's on Fifth Avenue and outfitted him from head to foot with a full complement of clothes along with accessories and extras. Sanner's old clothes could have been bundled up and mailed back to Arkinda to use for scarecrows. When Sanner appeared in the lobby of the Bear Mountain Inn, the epitome of splendor and elegance, even Leo Durocher—himself one of the leaders in the dress parade—had to admire his appearance and run a finger over the luxurious cloth.

Buzzie, you might say, had touched all the bases.

During my tenure with Rickey, I recall certain pronouncements or Rickeyisms that were among his favorites. I give them to you to decipher:

MAN'S EXTREMITY IS GOD'S OPPORTUNITY. He was always cautioning the managers not to make suggestions to the player when the player was doing well, because if the manager showered advice on a hitter who was hitting .300 and he would suddenly begin to level off to his normal batting average, the player was apt to blame the manager and say if he had been left alone he'd have had a good year. "Wait until the player is desperate and comes to you for help," he cautioned. He cited the case of Eddie Rickenbacker, floating on a raft after his crash in the South Pacific. In his extremity he began to pray to God and a rescue followed.

LUCK IS A RESIDUE OF DESIGN. By this Rickey meant that after you have made all your plans, taken advantage of your strength, the opposing team's weaknesses and have hustled one hundred per cent, whatever was left over was luck; that a player shouldn't complain about bad or good luck, because it was the residue of design. He reminded us that the harder one tried, the more luck one seemed to have.

THE PLEASING SKILLS OF THE FINISHED ATHLETE. This, Rickey said, was what the spectators came to see and what they enjoyed: the athlete who had beautiful coordination. He ofttimes compared infield practice to ballet where graceful players who had pleasing skills went through the pre-game practice.

THE AMERICAN PEOPLE WILL COME TO FIND THAT A BARE NECESSITY WILL BE A PLEASANT SUFFICIENCY. This was a phrase used during the War when he attended bond and enlistment rallies. It was in connection with the attempt to justify the continuation of professional baseball in those trying times of emotional stress and sacrifice.

THE ANESTHETIC BALLPLAYER. There were, he said, ballplayers who by their actions anesthetize the manager into thinking they are good players or better than they really are. He said that a boy will play half a dozen games badly, you'll take him out and put him in to pinch-hit and he might deliver a key blow—even a home run for you. Because of that you'll play him four or five more games

71

because he anesthetized you with that home run. When you decide that a player is not good enough to play frequently on your club, the best thing to do is to get rid of him because if you don't have him you can't use him.

GOOSE HUNTERS. This was derived from one of Rickey's hunting trips. He was shooting geese in his native state of Ohio and one of his companions mentioned that he had a nephew, an excellent ballplayer, and he thought he could make it. More to fulfill an obligation than because he believed it, Rickey invited him to spring training. When, later, we would be discussing various players in camp as to their weaknesses and strength, and where they could or couldn't play, Mr. Rickey, describing such a player, would say, "And now we come to our goose hunter." So anybody brought into camp on the recommendation of a politician or a friend was always referred to as a "goose hunter."

ADDITION BY SUBTRACTION. The expression was used relative to the bad ballplayer, the fellow who cannot help you. Rickey's advice was that as soon as you have made up your mind this man is of no use to you, the thing to do is to get rid of him, because as long as you have him around you'll be tempted to put him in to pinch-hit or pinch-run or finish out two or three innings in the field, and he'll hurt you. But if you don't have him around it will be impossible to play him. Then he is addition by subtraction.

LEISURE IS THE HANDMAIDEN OF THE DEVIL. Rickey in spring training continually impressed upon the manager and the scouts how important it was to keep ballplayers busy and would cite examples where, during days of idleness, a player got into trouble—subsequently costing his club the pennant.

COCONUT SNATCHING. "Over in Hawaii," Rickey explained, "they have those coconut palms. It's a simple matter to get people to collect the coconuts as they are cut from the tree, but they have difficulty getting the boys to climb the trees to do the snatching. What they do in that case is to take some of the fellows who are picking up the coconuts and make snatchers out of them.

"So what we'll have to do is this: we have an abundance of infielders. We'll have to take some of them and convert them into outfielders. In other words, we'll do some coconut snatching."

(Those familiar with the parlance of Casey Stengel may possibly understand the above.)

Frequently when Rickey held sway over an audience, he would, either by design or accident, do something offbeat or singularly odd that defied definition. A case in point occurred at a large auditorium we used in Vero Beach for movies and his lectures. Before a large captive audience of ballplayers he discoursed on the art of pitching. He analyzed the mechanics, the various techniques, the science, the refinements, putting his voice, heart, soul, and forty years of baseball learning into his talk.

Having exhausted the topic after an hour and a half, and perspiring freely, he reached into a side pocket, pulled forth a black silk sock and nonchalantly wiped his wet face with it.

The first time I sat with Rickey at a baseball game we were in spring training. It was an exhibition tussle between our Montreal and St. Paul clubs. After the St.

73

Paul hurler threw but one pitch, which was fouled off, Rickey tapped me on the shoulder.

"The pitcher's a bad fielder, the catcher blinks his eyes when the batter swings, and the center fielder gets a bad jump on the ball. Did you observe that?"

"No," I shook my head, "not on one pitch."

He explained his findings.

"The pitcher in letting go of the ball fell off the mound toward first base instead of coming to an even set position, which indicates he's a poor fielder. The ball was fouled over the catcher's right shoulder and he turned to the left. If he didn't blink he would have seen the ball come off the bat and know in which direction it went."

He paused.

"But what about the center fielder?" I asked.

Rickey continued: "Even though the ball did not come out toward center field, it was fouled off to one side and a good center fielder, when the hitter swings and the ball is fouled off in one direction, may not start in that direction but will sort of lean—that way he gets a good jump on the ball."

That was the beginning of eight years of a concentrated baseball education under the tutelage of a master. I had quit Columbia University to play professionally before I got a degree. But now I was working toward one. You could call it a B.R. (Branch Rickey) degree.

Along the road toward this mythical degree, Rickey called me into his Brooklyn office, informed me that it appeared very much as though he had to have another outfielder on the Dodgers if he wanted to win the pennant.

We always seemed short one capable outfielder. When the *Brooklyn Daily Eagle* closed its doors following a prolonged strike, New York sportswriters referred to Brooklyn as the largest city in the United States without a newspaper, a railroad station, or a left fielder. Even when we had formidable clubs from 1946 to 1955, we had trouble in left field. One year we had Carl Furillo, Duke Snider, and Andy Pafko. There were no complaints about this trio, but we traded Pafko, leaving a hole in left field. We tried to fill in with Dick Whitman, Gene Hermanski, Sandy Amoros, Don Thompson, and others. Whoever played this position never compared with the rest of the ball club, as we had fellows like Campanella, Hodges, Robinson, Reese, Cox, Snider, and Furillo.

"What about Marvin Rackley?" Rickey asked me. Rackley was a whiz at Montreal.

I volunteered, "I think Rackley is a pretty good ballplayer for a little fellow."

He gazed at me searchingly. "Do you know of any league that just uses little fellows?"

"No, sir," I answered.

"Alright then, begin again and tell me what kind of a ballplayer is Rackley?"

"Just fair and of doubtful major league ability," I summed him up.

Never again did I qualify any remark that I made about a player in talking to Rickey. He wanted no ifs, no ands, no buts, no conjecture. Only facts and your opinion.

Rickey called many meetings. Present at them all was Bob Finch, a kindly gentleman, one of his assistants, who would sit on the raised platform. Attending group meetings of scouts and managers discussing the talents of players, he continuously heard, "Brown can run like a sonofabitch. . . . Jones can throw like a sonofabitch. . . . Smith can field like a sonofabitch."

Then he went to a players' meeting. As he was leaving the hall he heard one young fellow ask another, "Who's that fat sonofabitch with the glasses perched on the edge of the platform?"

Finch realized he was the object of the inquiry. Instead of becoming angry he was elated.

"Now I've really made the team," he told everybody.

Once Rickey called a meeting of the scouts and minor league managers before we went to training camp. Some twenty-five of us together with front office personnel crammed his office. Midway in the meeting Rickey questioned Jake Pitler, who had managed the Newport News club in the Piedmont League, about a young pitcher.

"He looked real good in spring training and I can't understand why he didn't have a better year," Rickey wondered.

Jake had an excuse. "He started off real good, Mr. Rickey, and then he developed some arm trouble. It got sore and he wasn't able to take his turn."

Rickey mulled this over in his mind and asked, "Was it ossified?"

I was sitting behind Jake, who was hesitant in answering as he was grappling with the word "ossified." He opened his mouth. Nothing came out and a red blush crept up his neck.

Leaning over I whispered in his ear, "Tell him he doesn't touch a drop."

The blush disappeared and Jake called out, "Oh, no, Mr. Rickey," he defended his young ballplayer, "this boy never drank at all."

Rickey frowned at Pitler and admonished, "Jake, I

suggest at future meetings that you sit somewhere besides in front of Thompson."

When Branch Rickey sprang his coup d'état in 1946 and brought Jackie Robinson, the first Negro in the major leagues, to play for the Dodgers, Rickey was hailed as the Great White Father who broke the color line. He received all the credit.

Right here I want to set the record straight.

While it might have been Rickey's original idea to find a place for Robinson on the team, he was only a 25 per cent stockholder in the organization. The move would not have been possible without the permission of the other stockholders: Walter O'Malley, Jim Mulvey, and John Smith.

Neither Robinson nor Rickey ever mentioned the co-operation they received and the sanction in carrying out this plan.

CHAPTER 5

THE MOST TRAVELED MAN
ON THE CLUB

I BEGAN working for Mr. Rickey as a scout within our own organization. Mr. Rickey felt that the field manager would be so close to his team that he couldn't see the forest for the trees. Someone else who came in and sat up in the grandstand would have a different perspective. After sitting in the stand I'd go to dinner with the manager or meet him after the game and tell him where he was hurting. Either the shortstop wasn't covering as much ground as he should, or the center fielder was getting a bad jump on balls hit into his territory, or the infielders were playing in improper positions, or perhaps his team was top-heavy with left-hand hitters and he needed some right-handed power.

Mr. Rickey termed this TEAM BALANCING.

Only on special assignments did my scouting encompass the scouting of free-agent players. If I discovered a player who showed promise of developing into a major-leaguer, Rickey would be most anxious for the youngster to get married, reasoning that married life should prove a stabilizing influence and lessen the moral and physical risk. Mr. Rickey, a strong family man himself, believed in togetherness long before the word became popularized.

Nevertheless, his dogma did not prevent his dispatching me on special scouting assignments two successive Thanksgivings, a particularly important family day to me. One of these safaris was to Havana, Cuba, and the other to Caracas, Venezuela, separating me from my loved ones by many miles. In neither country could I describe or pronounce what I ate on this American holiday but the pains from gastronomical disturbances are just beginning to disappear after these many years.

The Venezuelan trip was the more adventurous. Rickey concealed the name of the player whom he wished scouted. "You go down there with an open mind and you'll find him," was all he said.

In Venezuela they had a winter baseball league, the roster dotted with the names of American boys. Arriving in Caracas, I retired early and was awakened by what I thought were car backfires. They weren't. They were shots. I glanced out the window, saw a few people running hither and yon. The next morning I went to the newsstand to buy an American newspaper and saw across the front of all the Spanish language newspapers, in large type, the word: SUSPENDIDO.

I approached the bilingual desk clerk for a translation, inquiring, "What gives with this *Suspendido?*"

Finishing stamping a letter, he calmly answered, "During the night we changed governments. A revolution. Everything is suspended: the right of free assembly, radio stations, newspapers. Martial law exists and no one is allowed on the streets from 9:00 P.M. until 6:00 A.M. without a special police permit."

79

I asked, "What about baseball games?"

"*Suspendido!*"

The revolutionary party moved swiftly into office and two nights later baseball was resumed. It was quite obvious that the player Mr. Rickey wanted me to scout was an American Negro, Jim Pendleton, from Chicago. Jim, I learned, was the property of the Chicago American Giants of the Negro National League. During this scouting expedition under the most unusual circumstances, I was also able to sign another player, "Chico" Carrasquel, who later played for us at Fort Worth and Montreal and whom Rickey sold to the Chicago White Sox for a sizable sum.

Scouting is the life blood of a major league organization. Any organization which expects to remain competitive must have a capable, industrious, and adventurous scouting staff. The major league scout must have three qualifications: detective, bloodhound, and diplomat. He must have nerve, strong arches, and a crystal ball. Major league clubs own or subsidize their own farm systems. This calls for many scouts and the constant unearthing of new talent for replacements, much like the worn-out parts of an old car, are continually needed. After great careers with the Dodgers, men like Reese after sixteen years, Snider after fifteen years, Hodges after sixteen years, Furillo after fourteen years, and Erskine after fourteen years must be replaced. The King is dead! Long live the King!

In a major-league organization there are two types of scouts: first is the free agent or "production" scout. He produces the green, untried player who must be developed through the farm system. He's the man you'll see at American Legion contests, high schools, colleges, sandlots, and perhaps some day in the future at the Little League games, warding off proud parents singing the praises of phenoms. His efforts are directed toward the grass roots of baseball, where he finds the free-agent player; the boy who has never played professionally but who is well-coached in questing for the big bonus with dollar signs for eye pupils.

The "production" scout examines these boys to determine whether he can fit any of them into our minor league organization and to judge whether they have the potential to become good professional ballplayers. The success of a major league organization hinges on the industry and judgment of the "production" scouts.

The other type scout is called the "club" scout. He is generally older and more experienced. These scouts spend the majority of their time scrutinizing other National and American League clubs and their top minor league teams. Occasionally they'll tour the spring training camps of the other clubs because the personnel on other clubs, just as on ours, changes constantly. They'll appraise the new hitters and the young pitchers and report back to our manager that this fellow is a high- or low-ball hitter and that some youngster has a fine curve that he uses in a jam. With this information these new players will not be complete strangers when we meet them for the first time during the championship season.

As the police department might say, "We have a file on him."

Scouting can be distilled into a single sentence: the business of looking for new talent and looking at other people's new and old talent. The Dodgers spend about $160,000 yearly in salaries of scouts, plus approximately

$100,000 in traveling expenses. Outright cash bonuses to young players call for an outlay of some $400,000. Our Vero Beach training camp costs $250,000 to operate. Losses at our Spokane ownership club and the subsidizing of our other minor league affiliations run to $250,000. All of these items are charged to replacements for the continued operation of the Los Angeles Dodgers.

Just as it takes some time to learn whether or not a player is going to make the grade, so it takes time to find out a scout's value. That is because it takes time for the youngsters signed by the scout to reach their "leveling off" stage. Some scouts are conservative in their estimates of players and others are high. A few years of reading their reports and seeing players whom they have signed, and you can catalog the scout.

Scouts leave one club and come to another because of a change in administration, difficulties with their front offices, or because of increased salary. There's no more permanency to a scouting job than there is to any other branch of baseball. If you want to make a down payment on a house at the base of your operations, the risk is entirely yours.

Scouting is hard work and a scout expects nothing in the way of gratitude from any of his hopefuls who reach the majors. At first he may receive a "thanks" from the player, but should the player become a star, the attitude may change to: "That scout took a long time to sign me." Or he may come up with a complaint that the scout gave him a very poor bonus to sign his first contract. This is a frequent lament, even though the Dodger scout's offer was the best and possibly the only bonus offer he received.

Rarely is a scout able to go hunting or fishing. Many

have difficulty retaining a faint recollection of members of their immediate families. It is a twenty-four hour daily job during the baseball season and in the off season. He must also put up a good front—exuding personality—on his travels. It's friends, and lots of them, that not only help a scout but actually make him successful. No single scout could possibly see all of the games played in his territory, so he has to depend on his friends for tips on the better boys. This is known as "institutionalizing" a territory. These friends are called "bird dogs" because they flush up the good talent which the regular scout might never see. If these fellows skip him and tip off someone else, chances are that there will be another scout working that territory very shortly.

Unquestionably, the scout is the most traveled man in an organization. We have scouts in Texas and the Middle West who travel 70,000 or 80,000 miles in their cars, a test of any stomach, as well as other parts of the anatomy. City scouts might not travel as many miles, but they're on the move just as much and in heavier traffic.

A scout, in most cases, goes to see the ballplayers, but in some instances they come to him. That happens when a major league club runs "tryout camps" in different sections of the country. The "tryout camp" receives a lot of advance publicity and youngsters come in from the surrounding territory with stars in their eyes. We usually have several scouts and occasionally I attend these "tryout camps" to grade these hopefuls. Due to the extensive scouting by all major league organizations, this type of camp has lost a great part of its value. Several present-day major leaguers just walked into "tryout camps" hoping to be signed to a contract.

What do we look for? It's no secret—all scouts look for

the same traits in youngsters. There are few hard and fast rules about scouting. If there were, almost anyone could be an acceptable scout just by following the rules. A truly successful scout is a combination of many things: experience, imagination, patience, industry, perseverance, and common sense. All scouts have their own methods of appraisal and their own manner of reaching conclusions. Scouts keep these ways and manners to a certain degree flexible. I would like to mention some of the things that scouts must search for in players—always with the caution that because professional baseball is played by physically exceptional men, it is the exceptional which you are seeking, and in such a search it is often wise to throw away the book.

We all realize that American Legion, high school, and even some college players have not yet reached their maturity. This compels us to look into and weigh potentials when judging the prospective player. Certain talents of a boy of seventeen or eighteen are already established and will develop very little. Other talents can and may expand over the years if his present actions do not violate any of the basic fundamentals. The scout must decide which talents are already here to stay and which are likely to appear as the youngster matures.

Many skills required by a professional baseball player are more often potential than actual in the youngster. Appraising these skills requires keen judgment and powers of clairvoyance. But certain fundamentals in the performance of baseball—particularly in hitting and fielding—cannot be violated. Some faults and ineptitudes are beyond salvation. A scout must not butt his head against a stone wall in his efforts to see what isn't there.

Running speed is an asset immediately apparent.

Teaching players to keep their eyes straight ahead on their objective and the use of proper knee action may increase their running speed slightly. But again, we know that nothing—neither coaching nor maturity—will turn a lead-footed boy into a Maury Wills. Running speed is placed first because it is the only talent used on offense and defense. The good runner can beat out bunts, infield hits, and take the extra base, and can also move quicker in the field pursuing the batted ball. From the crack of the bat until the foot strikes first base, the average time for a right-hand hitter is four seconds; for a left-hander, close to three and eight-tenths.

Scouts can be deceived by running speed. It requires close study. The little short-legged fellow who pumps his legs like pistons will, at first, appear to be flying. The tall, long-legged fellow with the loping stride seems not to move as fast, yet in a race would breast the tape far in advance of his diminutive opponent. The scout, by carrying a stopwatch, avoids guesswork. Lack of running speed can be overlooked in pitching prospects and, if other abilities are exceptional, in first basemen and catchers.

The first taste of beer, the first whiff of steaming, brewing coffee, the first sniff of a freshly opened can of pipe tobacco is always the best, and this goes for the first view of a young prospect's throwing arm. It can be measured solely by what he shows you. You cannot hope for marked improvement. You may teach him to take fewer steps with the ball, and make him throw lower, but nothing can be done to increase velocity. You gauge the velocity of the throw and check closely whether the ball takes off when it hits the ground or whether it seems to die. There are very few positions that can be played, and none that can be played well, if your arm is below average.

Hitting is judged on form. Notice whether or not a player violates the fundamentals of hitting: short stride, still bat, solidly planted rear foot, no fear of the pitched ball, and no turn of the head before meeting the ball. Good hitters and potentially good hitters observe all of these basic fundamentals.

Some faults, however, are correctable in a youngster with reasonable aptitude. There is hope for the head swinger—the boy who turns his head as he starts his swing and tries to hit from memory; for the wild swinger—the player who does not know the strike zone and cannot or will not wait for a strike to hit; and the boy who uppercuts and does not swing level at the ball. All of the above hitting faults are correctable with practice and more practice. Fear of the pitched ball—afraid that you will be hit with the ball—is extremely hard to correct. Courage is a difficult attribute to instill in anyone.

Power—the extra base hit—can come to a youngster as he develops physically, providing he has the frame for more size and more weight. Sometimes a look at the boy's parents will indicate to you how much more he will develop. Putting together these observations, coupled with what you expect the player to gain in strength and physique, should furnish a good lead on his possible power.

Fielding, basically, is good form exhibited through grace and rhythm. Prime essentials are a "live" body, strong legs, and a capable, flexible pair of hands. You can put in a thimble the awkward, ungraceful athletes who have become smooth fielders. If the infielder keeps his head down as he approaches the ground ball, with knees slightly bent, and his arms give a trifle with the ball, you are watching an A-1 fielder. Fielding is a very important part of this game of baseball, regardless of the general opinion of the press and the ordinary fan. A player wears his glove for eight or nine innings of a ball game, but goes to bat only three or four times in the average game. With these odds it should be quite obvious that a ragged fielder has more opportunities to hurt a club than a good hitter has to drive in a few runs.

Scouting outfielders is somewhat simpler than other positions, mainly because of the limitations of their duties. The fielding ability of these "men of swat" is of more significance than the fans realize. Should an infielder boot one, it generally means only one extra base, as the outfielder is behind him to back up. If an outfielder misses one, it can result in two or three bases, for nothing is behind him but fences.

An outfielder needs good speed and a strong throwing arm. He needs a good jump on fly balls. He needs range. If a ball is batted to the outfield and you turn your head toward the fielder and see him start for the ball, you can write him off as a poor fielder. He should be in high gear pursuing the batted ball before you turn to see him make the play.

Outfielders are mostly the power men on the club. They not only are expected to hit for a respectable average, but should contribute the occasional long ball.

An outfielder with a mediocre arm can squeeze by in left field if he has sure hands and a potent bat. This same type arm would prove disastrous in center or right field— base runners would go from first to third on a single and score from second with little danger of being thrown out at the plate.

The second baseman and shortstop need not hit as much as the other regulars. His fielding, though, has to be nearly flawless. The outfielder has fewer fielding opportunities, therefore his lapses with the glove are forgiven in proportion to how frequently and often and far he clubs the ball.

Pitchers are easiest to judge. This is borne out by the large number of pitchers signed in comparison to the total number of players signed for other positions. Although it is easier to judge pitchers, it is equally easy to make mistakes in determining which have major league possibilities. Run-of-the-mill baseball fans can view a young pitcher and say, "That kid can throw hard. He has a chance to be a fine pitcher." Close scrutiny, however, is necessary to tell whether or not the ball is alive. There are so many intangibles in the makeup of a pitcher that we must be careful in order not to be misled by a first impression. Along with stuff, or pitching equipment, pitchers must have stamina, aptitude, determination, and HEART. Without these qualities, the good fast ball and the sharp curve are valueless.

Scouts search for the good, fast ball from a young pitcher because that is the God-given talent with which most pitchers who become successful begin. We cannot teach the youngster to throw hard, but we are presumptuous enough to think that we can teach the prospect control, the curve ball, the change of pace, and other refinements of the pitching art.

I do not mean to imply that a scout would turn his back on a youngster just because he doesn't have a blazing fast ball. If he has a good curve, good control, and good changes of speed, he can still become a successful major league pitcher. There have been many pitchers who got by in the majors without the exceptional fast ball, such as Stu Miller, Warren Spahn, Carl Hubbell, and Ted

Lyons, to name a few. Those who have done it largely on an exceptional fast ball alone—pitchers like Walter Johnson, Van Lingle Mungo, Bob Feller, and Lefty Grove—you can name on the fingers of your two hands.

A pitcher can fool the hitter in two ways. He may fool the hitter by a variation of plane in the delivery of the ball toward home plate. For this he uses a curve, knuckler, slider, screwball, or a live fast ball that rises or sinks. He may also fool the hitter by a change in the velocity of the pitch, causing the ball to reach the batter sooner or later than he anticipates. This is done by an overpowering fast ball which he literally blows by the hitter before he expects it or by varying the speed of the pitch with the same motion and getting the ball to the hitter after he expects it and after he has committed his stride.

The specter of the sore arm is always looking over the scout's shoulder when he signs a pitcher. The Dodgers had three of the finest pitching prospects of the last twenty years—Rex Barney, Jack Banta, and Karl Spooner —become worthless due to arm injuries.

Great care must be exercised in the scouting of catchers. Good catchers are scarce items. No one wants to catch because, first of all, it is hard work; secondly, it is dangerous. Catchers do not wear the mask, shinguards, and chest protector just to appear like a man from Mars. These and other safety devices are the necessary, if insufficient, protection from foul tips, low pitches, and sliding base-runners. Other players call all of this equipment "the tools of ignorance." They dispute the fact that so-and-so is a smart catcher. They argue that if he were smart he never would have become a catcher.

The catcher, like the pitcher, is truly a specialist. Infielders can play the outfield and outfielders can play the infield acceptably in an emergency, but no one but a catcher can catch. The catcher must be rugged, intelligent, and a "take charge guy." He's the quarterback of the baseball nine. He must have a strong, quick arm and a strong, sure pair of hands. Young catchers can be taught to shift for pitches, to catch pop fouls, the proper way to throw and how to tag, so we do not look for these proficiencies in the young fellow.

In the scouting setup, there are full-time scouts and part-time scouts. The full-timer is on the payroll for twelve months a year and available for assignments—to Puerto Rico, the Dominican Republic, or Venezuela— at all times. Part-time scouts work only during the baseball season and sometimes then only on weekends. These men are generally retired ballplayers, pensioners, fans, or simply baseball buffs looking to make an extra buck doing work that they enjoy. Many of these part-time men are hopeful that some day they'll come up with the star that will earn for them a full-time scouting job.

Part-time scouts are important because they often uncover a really great player. It was a volunteer fireman who spotted the potential in Mickey Mantle. The fireman sent Mantle from his home in Commerce, Oklahoma, to the Yankees farm club in Joplin, Missouri, for a tryout. Johnny Sturm, the Joplin manager, who had played some first base for the Yankees, saw Mantle's possibilities and told him to do nothing until he heard from the Yankees after his graduation from high school. On graduation day Mickey barely had time to untie the ribbon on his diploma before Tom Greenwade, the Yankee scout in that area, offered him a Class D contract in the Yankee organization and a bonus of about $1,000, which Mantle signed. In such strange and wondrous ways are baseball bargains found.

An almost equally good buy was the Yankees' rookie sensation of 1951, Gil McDougald. When he played high school ball in San Francisco, all but one of the ivory hunters in that area shied away from him because of his unorthodox stance at the plate. They were fearful of the manner in which he draped the bat over his right wrist as though it were too heavy. The late Joe Devine, of the Yankee scouting staff, disregarded what we call a "preliminary" stance, deciding it made no difference how the boy held the bat before the pitcher released the ball. More important, Devine correctly maintained, was the player's ability to have the bat ready to swing when the pitcher delivered the ball. McDougald had that ability, as the pitchers in the American League would agree.

McDougald was anxious to play pro baseball and would have signed with any of those reluctant scouts for perhaps $600. Devine gave him $1,500, probably because Gil made Devine's spine "tingle a little." Joe may have said to himself, "Well, I'll gamble $1,500 on this boy. He has a chance to become a fine ballplayer."

But scouts "gambling" must remember that they are doing it with money that isn't their own, so caution is one of the qualities we look for in a scout. If he doesn't exercise a degree of caution he can break you financially.

Supposing that any one scout had access in the last five years to every youngster who received $50,000 or more to sign and this fictitious scout had said "no" to all these players. Naturally, he would have saved his club a lot of money, as there have been several $50,000 lemons signed during that period.

If this had happened, you wouldn't have Frank Howard, Carl Yastrzemski, Tim McCarver, or Dick Ellsworth, to mention a few topnotch players who received high bonuses for their signatures. Still, there were some two million dollars spent on players who tried for a few years to hit the "optical illusion (curve ball)" and then wired home, "Shine up the dinner pail, Mom, they're starting to curve me."

It's easy to get yourself scouts who can sign boys to contracts. Many of them sign a lot of boys but the youngsters aren't away from home long enough to be missed. These scouts sweep clean, just as though they were handling a broom. But their winning percentage is very low. Which do you think would be the better scout, the man who signs four boys of whom two make good, or the man who signs twenty, none of whom make good?

It's as simple as that. Yet, in the face of all of this, Branch Rickey felt that in quantity a scout would find quality. It is difficult to fault the kind of success that Mr. Rickey achieved. I can only say that, in the face of the huge bonuses that are paid today, such scouting would bankrupt any club.

If a young man feels inclined to get into the scouting field he can be self-trained. No course offered in any college curriculum is going to help, as no degrees are needed. He will have to study the raw material and compare them to players he has seen in the majors, making the necessary adjustments for age and experience. If he fully understands what is required of a ballplayer he can teach himself to look for the necessary qualifications, even though he has never played anything but sandlot ball himself. He must be able to "size up" a boy and say, "There's a fellow who does it the way it should be done."

He must be able to see that there are no obvious flaws

in the way a prospect plays, and that he doesn't violate any of the basic fundamentals of his position. The wishful scout must be able to state with confidence, "Here's a player who five years from now will be a possible major leaguer."

You have checked and rechecked the player's ability and have liked everything you could see. What about the things you can't see? If you could just look "under the hood" to see what makes him tick you would be home free. Strange as it may seem, we find youngsters who can hit, run, field, and throw, but you can't mix all of the ingredients and come up with a ballplayer. They can't stand the pressure, they don't have the desire to play, so they just stumble along and never reach the heights that their potential indicated they would attain.

The player being observed by the would-be scout might be striking out at the time he is under scrutiny. He might look like a monkey wrestling a coconut on every ground ball hit to him, but this can be corrected. Suppose you're fairly certain that a boy whom you are watching has possibilities, but that you are on no one's payroll. What's the next step?

You submit a detailed report to the big-league club of your choice, and if he has not been scouted previously by that club, the chances are that a regular scout from that organization will be sent out to inspect him. If the scout's judgment bears out yours, and the boy is signed to a contract—well, you're on your way to a scouting career. If your boy makes good, his signing will tide you over a few mistakes until you get your feet on the ground.

After that it's up to you. But your initial break can be made by writing a letter. I know. I wrote one applying for a job in the minors forty-one years ago.

CHAPTER 6

THE MALIGNED GENTLEMEN
IN BLUE

Some years ago, when Sigmund Freud furnished us with a new vocabulary and no one was called just plain crazy any more but had his or her abnormalities identified by a fancy name, I considered following the signs of the times and writing a book based on the most gigantic decision in the life of a fictitious umpire.

Setting was the Yankee Stadium during the World Series. Contestants were the Yankees and Dodgers. It was the final game, last of the ninth, score tied, the count three and two on the Yankee batter.

The pitcher released the ball. The batter didn't swing and it plunked into the catcher's glove.

Ball? Or strike?

Sixty-six thousand spectators waited for a sign from the umpire.

He merely shook his head.

After a cordon of police escorted him through hostile crowds to the safety of the Stadium office and the Commissioner of Baseball and others of high position faced him, the room grew silent.

"Just try to tell me what happened," the Commissioner encouraged.

The umpire had a broad, honest face. He held his head high, faced the group and said in a low, clear voice:

"Gentlemen, the pitch was too close to call. It could have gone either way. It was a momentous decision for me to make. In all fairness, I simply could not call it a ball or a strike."

After this beginning I would flash back into the formative years of this beleaguered umpire and, from a chain of events originating from early environment, probe until the reason was discovered why the man in blue couldn't make up his mind.

In the final chapter the umpire would break the trauma by making an important decision that was to save a human life.

Well, I had a suspenseful beginning and an ending that justified the shirking of his earlier responsibility. All I lacked were about 300 double-spaced typewritten pages in between.

This plot recurrently comes to mind as I sit high in Dodger Stadium, marveling at the deportment of the umpires below, handling the game with the authority of supreme beings.

As a player and manager I rode umpires like a cowboy rides a steer at a rodeo, and I got tossed just as much. You can't beat 'em and you can't join 'em. There are only two groups of people in the world who have the last word: umpires and wives, and if you dispute either you can get thrown out of a game or your comfortable home with equal speed.

Seeing that umpires have the final word, and supplemented by the fact that their adrenalin isn't rushing as fast as yours because you exploded first, the closing remarks made by them before you head for the clubhouse and an early shower are the result of clearer thinking.

When Burt Shotton managed at Philadelphia he had a long-winded argument with umpire Bill Klem, one of the better known of the breed.

Shotton's closing line was: "Klem, you just plain stink!"

Klem fired back: "Alright, Shotton, suppose you go into the clubhouse and see how I smell from there."

While I was in the National League we had an umpire named Charley Moran, who was also the football coach of Center College in Kentucky, nicknamed the "Praying Colonels." Center College made headlines the year Harvard signed them on their schedule as a breather, but when the final gun sounded it was the Crimson who were on the losing end, gasping for breath.

I was on second base and a ball was hit to the outfield. Leaving second with the idea of scoring, I rounded third and the catcher, the ball, Charley Moran, and I met in a cloud of dust at home plate. I got up, started brushing myself off, positive I'd scored the run.

Moran harbored contradictory thoughts.

We began arguing. At length I said, "I understand you coach football at Center College."

"I do," he said pleasantly, "and we have a good team."

"And aren't they known as the Praying Colonels?"

He said they were.

"Now I know why they prayed before every game when you coached," I cracked.

He said, "Alright, Son, since you turned the conversation to religious channnels, suppose you get into the clubhouse and baptize yourself."

George Moriarty, an umpire who later managed the Chicago White Sox, was officiating an exhibition game between the Dodgers and Detroit. There was a young rookie batting for the Tigers and the Dodger pitcher threw one on the corner that might have gone either way.

Moriarty indicated a strike.

The indignant rookie jerked his head around and for ten seconds stared straight at Moriarty.

"Hey, Kid," Moriarty warned, "don't you turn around and stare at me until you earn your spurs in the big leagues."

The rookie apologized. "I'm sorry, Mr. Moriarty," he said meekly, "but I was just wondering how you spell your name."

The umpire carefully spelled out M-o-r-i-a-r-t-y.

"Just as I thought—one 'i'," the youngster said.

Intimidation of an umpire in the majors is unheard of. Once I saw it happen in a semi-pro game. A little fellow was umping and a strapping six foot, four inch star outfielder, a local favorite, came up. The count was one ball, one strike. On the next pitch the umpire cried, "Two!"

The giant swung toward him menacingly, demanding, "Two what?"

"Too low, play ball," the umpire said hurriedly.

No official in any United States spectator sport is subjected to the crowd abuse received by an umpire. Day after day and night after night, vilifications bombard him. "Thief, robber, bum, idiot," rain down upon him from the stands, and before beer and soft drinks were poured into paper cups to safeguard his skull, bottles came hurtling his way. If there were a full set of lyrics and a tune to go with them, "Kill the Umpire!" might lead the popular song parade.

Many of the umpires have a quick wit, yet unfortunately their release of it reaches only a few arguers. An exception occurred on a barnstorming trip the Dodgers made to Japan in 1956.

Jackie Robinson was at bat, with runners on second and third. The Japanese pitcher worked the count to three balls and two strikes. Seemingly in a dilemma, the pitcher and catcher conferred at the mound. Both shrugged and looked at the bench. The manager held up four fingers pointing to first base, signifying he wanted his battery to give an intentional base on balls to Jackie Robinson and take their chances on the next hitter.

This tableau was played in rather slow motion and Robinson clearly witnessed the sign. Relaxing at the plate, he waited for the expected wide, outside pitch that would provide him with a free passage to first base.

Much to Jackie's amazement, the pitcher threw a fast ball right down the middle, splitting the plate for the third strike. Robinson had been tricked.

Jocko Conlan pulled off his mask and yelped to our dugout, "Hey, boys! Another Pearl Harbor."

Maury Wills, a flash of lightning on the base paths, supplied much extra work for the umpires. The year he set a new record for steals—104 in 1962—no umpire could risk taking his eyes off Maury for a second.

Against the Giants in Candlestick Park on one of those days when Alvin Dark had neglected to flood the base paths in order to slow down the fleet Dodger runners, Maury jetted toward second. Dusty Bogess made the umpire's motion meaning that Maury was out but at the same time said to Maury, "You're safe!"

Standing on the bag, the fastest Dodger of them all addressed Bogess. "Dusty, am I out or safe? Your thumb indicated that I was out, but I heard your voice say safe. Which is it?"

Dusty replied, "Maury, only you and these two Giants," pointing to José Pagan and Charles Hiller, "heard me call you safe, but 40,000 Giant fans saw me call you out. So, Maury, you're out!"

The power of an umpire is executed more swiftly than any wheels of justice spin in the courtrooms. It is indisputable, and although an appeal can be made, that still leaves you in the showers taking an early bath on the day it happened. In this land of the free and the home of the umpire baiters where democracy rules the roost, the player giving vent to his feelings realizes what life would be like under a dictatorship. The umpire doesn't even have to open his mouth. A jerk of the thumb can send a player off the field.

Irate fans sometimes scream, "Why don't you read the rules!"

Make no mistake about it, the umpire not only reads the rules, he digests them after thorough mastication. He eats them for breakfast, lunch, dinner. Some umps carry the rule book in hip pockets; others in their heads.

No certain physical build is necessary in the qualifications for umpiring. They can be fashioned like the side of a brick wall or appear to be a fugitive from a Nazi prison camp. As long as they have integrity, impartiality, don't let minds wander and keep their eyes on the ball, they are rivets securing the sides of the great American game together.

A disparity in size of the Mutt and Jeff variety was clearly visible the time PeeWee Reese argued with umpire George Magerkurth. Magerkurth stood six four, weighed 235; Reese was five eight, weighed 165.

On a close play at second, Reese tagged the runner and gazed up at Magerkurth, who called, "Safe!" PeeWee stood on tiptoe, making sure his voice carried to Magerkurth and Magerkurth stooped over Reese so he wouldn't miss anything.

The jaws of both men worked like pistons.

Finally Magerkurth had heard enough.

"Reese, if you don't shut up I'm going to bite your head off."

"Well, George," Reese snapped, "if you do you'll have more brains in your belly than you've got in your head."

During my managing days at Montreal there was an International League umpire I've previously mentioned, named Chuck Solodare, who held two jobs. He also officiated in the National Basketball League. Working in back of home plate, in my judgment he made a couple of bad decisions on sliding plays, besides missing a ball and strike here and there. Three times I went from the bench to argue with him. We were playing Jersey City in their park.

The bench in the Jersey City park was situated quite a distance from the plate, yet within range of my basso profundo. Just before I stepped into the dugout I trumpeted a final verbal blast.

Solodare jerked off his mask, booming, "You're through! You can go!"

This was the period when everybody was getting physical exams for Selective Service. I went up to Solodare and said angrily: "That's just your trouble. You've got

1-A ears and 4-F eyes. You hear everything everybody has to say but you don't see half the things you're supposed to see."

It was a nice shower.

Bucky Harris, manager of the Yankees in those days of international conflict, asked umpire Bill McGowan on the opening day of the season, "Bill, how do you think baseball will get through the war?"

McGowan wasn't sure. "I don't know," he said, "your guess is as good as mine."

"I know it is," Bucky said, satisfied with the answer, "but this is the first time you ever admitted it."

At Birmingham I got into an argument with the late Steamboat Johnson, the most colorful of the boys in blue down in Dixie. He lectured me: "Young man, this year's your first year in the league. Me and my partner out there at second base have been workin' around here for twenty years."

I asked sweetly, "Don't you think it's about time you and your partner got into some other business? You seem to be in a rut."

I think Steamboat was set to throw me out of the game but he looked at my face and saw a broad smile and allowed me to stay.

Eight years ago I picked up a book: "Bury Me in an Old Press Box," by Fred Russell, veteran and widely respected sportswriter for the *Nashville Banner*. I discovered that Fred had mentioned me. He wrote:

> One of the champions in the wisecracking department is Lafayette Fresco Thompson, vice-president in charge of the Brooklyn Dodgers' farm clubs, who also served in the Southern Association as manager at Birmingham and New Orleans. But the first time I saw Fresco he was a utility in-

101

fielder with the Giants, passing through Nashville for an exhibition. Late in the game, Frank Snyder, coaching at first, told Thompson to go in as a pinch runner.

"Thank you, Frank," he said, "but I've just had my shoes shined."

Very shortly thereafter, Thompson was through as a major-leaguer.

As Birmingham manager Fresco coached at third base and, when irritated beyond the legal limit by a persistent heckler, would go over and inquire the name of the man's undertaker.

"I want your head," he would say, "for my rock garden."

Thompson had Birmingham in the thick of the pennant race in 1938, but the club slumped, and I suppose it was the sight of the gay one in a fretful mood which prompted a delicate gag at his expense on a hot night in Nashville near the end of the season. A goodly crowd was on hand and behind the plate was a fat, noticeably nervous young umpire freshly promoted from the Southeastern League.

Although Birmingham grabbed an early lead, it didn't keep Thompson from riding the new umpire from the very first inning. He would sit on the concrete steps of the visiting club's dugout and direct a steady flow of uncomplimentary remarks which could be heard plainly up in the press box.

The idea occurred that Fresco should be sent a note, so a dainty missive was written in feminine backhand style and dispatched via the press box messenger boy who, in delivering it, remarked that "a lady back there in the box seats said to give this to you."

It read:

"Dear Mr. Thompson: I drove all the way from Dothan, Alabama today to see my nephew umpire his first Southern League game and I will appreciate it very much if you will quit saying such ugly things to him.
                    Lou Ella Brown"

After reading the note, Fresco folded it up, put it in his hip pocket, and immediately ceased his banter. For almost three innings he said nothing to the umpire.

Came the seventh, and Nashville put on a rally, going one run ahead. Birmingham came back the next round and had runners on first and second with none out, but on a single to center field the runner on second was thrown out on a very close play at the plate.

The player, jumping up in a cloud of dust as the umpire signaled him out, protested so that he was ejected from the game. Thompson raved and ranted, kicked dirt over home plate, all but pushed the new umpire, making quite a scene and barely escaping being chased. When he finally returned to his seat on the steps his abuse of the umpire was worse than ever. Surely Fresco had forgotten about the umpire's "dear old aunt" up on the stands who had driven over 450 miles for this occasion.

It was time to send another note.

In the same handwriting, and delivered by the same boy, the message went on its way. As Thompson received and unfolded same, it read:

"Mr. Thompson: If you don't stop insulting my nephew, I'm going to come down there and kick you in the (censored).

LOU ELLA BROWN"

Fresco rolled right off the top step and hit smack on the ground. He stayed there flat on his back until players rushed from the Birmingham dugout and lifted him, brushed off his uniform, and asked if he wanted a doctor. He said nothing, just handed them the note.

They read it and seemed to understand what a shock it had been for their manager.

For the rest of the season and on into the Winter, Fresco was telling about this strange experience—what an impulsive, bitterly outspoken lady fan he had encountered—and it wasn't until three years later that a confession was made to him.

In the Southern Association, while managing the New Orleans Pelicans, Billy Evans, the President of the league, told me he was taking on a young umpire, Danny Dever. Evans showered accolades on his new man. He had been up at the Great Lakes Naval Training Station.

Observing him work in our league I was inclined to agree with Evans. Then, after only one month, I noticed a letdown. Once established, he started to coast a little, not bearing down. In the process of an argument with him concerning calls in back of the plate, he stated, "I was umpiring at Great Lakes behind Bob Feller and Virgil Trucks, so I shouldn't have trouble with your pitchers."

"Yes," I retorted, "and the way you're umpiring today, you'll be behind trucks next year—only they'll be garbage trucks."

Managers, coaches, and players aren't the only ones embroiled with umps. The Dodgers were playing an exhibition game in North Carolina. A husky arbiter, Cy Rigler, was working home plate and behind him in a box seat sat an obstreperous fan, high as a kite on mountain dew.

Should Rigler holler, "Strike!" the fan thundered, "Ball!" If Rigler called, "Safe," he called, "Out!"

This continued unabated.

In the eighth inning Rigler leaned over to brush off the plate and when he straightened up found himself face to face with the perverse fan.

"You can't come down here. Get back in the stands!" Rigler ordered.

The fan stood swaying in front of him.

"Why, you're drunk," Rigler diagnosed, exclaiming, "I haven't seen anybody drunk as you in a long time."

Steadying himself, the reeling fan accused, "I may be drunk, but you're blind. You're the blindest ump I ever saw. Man, you're really blind."

Rigler took him by the arm, gently leading him to the stand and guiding him over a low railing into his box seat. The drunk smiled weakly at Rigler, causing the umpire to believe he must be a pretty good guy after all.

He complimented, "You're taking it in good spirit."

"That's all right—that's all right," the fan said thickly, "I told you you were blind and you told me I was drunk —but tomorrow I'll be sober and you'll still be blind."

As a player on the Dodgers I was on first base one day and got the steal-signal from the manager. On the next pitch I broke for the base, sliding into what I thought was a safe theft. Much to my surprise the umpire called me out.

I started an argument and in the course of it caught a whiff of his breath. It smelled of whiskey. This provoked the remark, "No wonder you blew the play."

"What do you mean by that?" he wanted to know.

"I mean I smell whiskey on your breath."

"Whiskey," he repeated, "why, I don't even touch the stuff."

"Well, I do," I told him, "and I certainly know how it smells."

No good umpire carries a grudge. He can't walk out on the field hoping to engage in a personal vendetta and think, "If Leo Durocher rides me from the coaching box today, I'm going to run him out of the game first chance I get." He must be without prejudice.

Players don't carry grudges either. Much as they may beef they realize the umpire has a hard, thankless, important job and that there's nothing personal in his decisions. Sure, he can be infrequently blocked out of play, but I've never seen an umpire call a play other than as it appeared to him.

There are certain umpires a player will bait more than others. Sometimes an innocent umpire becomes the target of all that has gone awry during the week: your batting average has fallen to .178; bills are coming due; that tiny boil on your rear never seems to heal, etc. So you release all your accumulated pent-up feelings on the poor umpire.

Bill Klem, one of the most proficient umpires the game ever knew, was a man I often squabbled with. He tossed me out of many a game, yet if I heard him criticized away from the park I would fight to defend his ability and fairness.

In 1929 Mel Ott of the Giants and Chuck Klein of the Phillies, with whom I was playing, entered the last day of the season tied for the home run leadership in the National League, with forty-two apiece. Klein clouted a homer his second time at bat in the first game of a doubleheader to take a 43-42 lead. Our pitchers, determined to protect their teammate so he could win the coveted honor, kept the ball outside, eventually walking Ott six times in the two games.

Klem kept objecting, declaring, "Poor sportsmanship. Ott should have a chance."

"Sportsmanship and ten cents will get you a cup of coffee," I scoffed.

A running controversy developed. As captain of the Phillies I felt I was expressing the opinions of my teammates.

I reminded Klem, "Our pitchers walked many men all year and this is the first time to my knowledge that you ever objected. Ott," I pointed out, "will get about

$40,000 even if he doesn't lead in home runs and Klein might get $10,000 if he finishes first in the home run derby."

Klem just snorted.

I should have quit when I was ahead. Instead I popped off, "Bill, you're supposed to be the umpire, but if you want to pull for Ott I suggest you go sit on the Giant bench."

"I have a suggestion for you," Klem replied.

"Yes, what is it?"

"I suggest, and strongly, that you retire to the clubhouse."

Burt Shotton, our manager, rushed out.

"What happened?" he asked.

I repeated to him what I'd told Klem.

Shotton thrust his face close to Klem's. "That goes for me too, Bill."

"Okay," Klem said, "in that case you can join Thompson for company on his way to the clubhouse."

We trudged to the showers together.

Only once did I torment Klem and get away with it. On the last day of the season the Dodgers and Giants were playing a doubleheader. The first game seemed to drag on forever but we finally beat them 11 to 8. It was 4:30 P.M. when the second game began. Pitching for the Giants was wild, hard-throwing lefthander Jim Mooney; for the Dodgers an equally wild and hard-throwing right-hander, Van Lingle Mungo. These two hurlers had been one-two in the Eastern League in strikeouts, bases on balls,—and hit batsmen.

As we reached the second inning the late September sky darkened and day began fading. Hitters on both sides were footloose and fancy free, executing steps worthy of

Arthur Murray, in their determination not to be struck by either of these scatter-arm pitchers and return to their families unscathed after their last game.

Alongside me on the bench pitcher Hollis Thurston dared me to go up to home plate and strike a match after a pitch, hoping Bill Klem would take the hint and call the game on account of darkness.

"I'll do better than that," I told Thurston, a plot forming in my mind, "just get me three or four scorecards."

He collected some and I rolled them together. As I trotted out to shortstop and picked up my glove, I lit one corner of the paper torch, turned my back and began to toss the ball around the infield. My fire was doing nicely. A buzz started through the stands as fans noticed the blaze. Klem always donned his mask with a majestic gesture of raising it high above his head with a sweeping motion. His hand stopped in mid-air as his eye caught the flames.

He strode out to me.

"Young man, did you light that fire?"

"What fire?" I asked, feigning surprise.

Klem said, "The one behind you."

I wheeled around and acted surprised. "Now who do you suppose would do a silly thing like that?" I said.

"I've got a pretty good idea," Klem grunted. He approached Dolly Stark, one of the base umps, inquiring whether or not he knew the identity of the firebug. Dolly shook his head.

I stamped out the remaining embers and Klem went back behind the plate. By now—due to the delay—it was so dark that Klem gave up trying to see the plate. The game was called.

Klem was adept at rolling with a verbal punch, parrying an insult, and cooling off the angry young men of baseball. Words never seemed to pierce his protective veneer to the point of pain. What hurt him most, I believe, in his many long years of umpiring, was the time the bespectacled Danny MacFayden, a Boston Brave pitcher, strolled slowly from mound to plate, removed his glasses, handed them to Klem, saying, "Here, Bill, you take these. You need them worse than I do."

League officials frown on umps and players socializing, traveling on the same plane, stopping at the same hotels. Nevertheless, a few players have climbed over the barriers and taken hunting trips with umpires. The result has proved the baseball players' true feelings for the men in blue.

No umpire has ever been shot.

CHAPTER 7

WALTER O'MALLEY TAKES OVER

In 1950 Walter O'Malley, a Brooklyn corporation lawyer, needed $1,050,000.

The Brooklyn Dodgers had refused to renew the contract of Branch Rickey as President and General Manager of the Dodgers. He advised that he was to become the General Manager of the Pittsburgh Pirates and was prepared to sell his stock in the Dodgers to William Zeckendorf, a financial tycoon, the President of Webb and Knapp, realtors.

The New Yorker had made the aforementioned offer.

Rickey owned 25 per cent of the stock, which he had purchased for approximately $365,000. The remaining 75 per cent was divided between O'Malley, James A. Mulvey and John L. Smith, deceased. O'Malley was representing Smith's widow, Mae Smith.

Under the agreement existing among the stockholders, the partners had the option of acquiring the stock of anyone who wanted out by meeting the highest bona fide offer.

O'Malley did not wish for any stock to go to an outsider, so he agreed to purchase Rickey's stock. O'Malley sold a couple of small companies he owned, plus stock in the Long Island Rail Road and the Brooklyn Union Gas Company, in order to make substantial down payments on Rickey's stock. O'Malley now owned 50 per cent of the stock and voted Mrs. Mae Smith's 25 per cent, so it was only natural that he become President of the club.

The Internal Revenue Department was in the middle of settling the taxes on John Smith's estate when the sale of Rickey's stock went through. The tax on his 25 per cent of the Dodger stock was being settled on the basis of the last sale of record: the purchase of 25 per cent by Rickey for $365,000. Now Uncle Sam called "Time" and asked for a recount. Mrs. Smith had to finally settle on the basis of the new value created by the sale of Rickey's stock. In the inheritance bracket of John Smith's estate, this turned out to be a sizable sum of money, so Rickey left two enemies in Brooklyn: Mrs. Mae Smith and Walter O'Malley, who felt that he had been sandbagged by Rickey.

O'Malley had one thing in common with Larry Mac-Phail and Branch Rickey. They were all portentous eaters and each harbored the same insatiable desire—to feast on the Yankees.

When Rickey departed for Pittsburgh to inaugurate his five year plan, it was believed he faced a serious problem. This was how to get rid of some of the players he had traded from Brooklyn to Pittsburgh over the past several years.

The new Dodgers under O'Malley were not lacking in talent. In 1949 Ed Fitzgerald, authoring one of the chapters of a book entitled *The Story of the Brooklyn Dodgers,* wrote:

Loaded to the gunwales with young, hustling ballplayers, the Dodgers look as though they'll be at or near the top for years to come. But one thing is a lead pipe cinch. Whether they win or whether they lose, whether they finish at the top or the bottom, the Dodgers will always be interesting.

One of O'Malley's first moves was to hire Charlie "Chuck" Dressen to replace Burt Shotton as field manager.

A change of front office personnel resulted and Buzzie Bavasi and I were appointed vice-presidents.

The 1951 team seemed a certain pennant winner as it moved into September with a comfortable lead. Robinson belted .338, Roy Campanella was close on his heels with .325, and Furillo, Reese, Snider, and Cox were all above .275. Hodges smashed forty home runs to break the club record held by "Babe" Herman.

In the pitching department Preacher Roe had a fantastic 22 wins with only 3 losses, Carl Erskine turned in 16 victories and Ralph Branca 13. Reliefer Clyde King contributed 14 wins and Clem Labine, who joined the club late, chalked up 5.

There was only one fly in the ointment. With a spectacular fall drive, the Giants tied the Dodgers, necessitating a play-off. With almost certain victory in the Dodgers' grasp, Bobby Thomson hit a long curving drive into the left field stands of the Polo Grounds, scoring Clint Hartung, running for Don Mueller, from third and Whitey Lockman from second, to give Leo Durocher's Giants the pennant and an opportunity to their manager, Superstitious Leo, to change the sox he had been wearing for many days while his club was in their stretch drive.

They called it "The Miracle of Coogan's Bluff."

O'Malley had suffered a crushing blow. Not long afterwards he attended a baseball meeting at the Waldorf-Astoria. When he boarded the elevator a Dodger sympathizer, not recognizing him, was crying to the elevator operator about how the Dodgers blew the pennant.

"Those jerks cost me fifty bucks," he moaned. "Fifty bucks! Think of that!"

Entering the conversation, O'Malley voiced his disappointment. "A terrible thing," he said solemnly.

"*You're* complaining," the passenger remarked. "How much did *you* lose?"

The elevator stopped at O'Malley's floor and the door swung open. Just before he left the car the President of the Dodgers said casually, "I figure it cost me between two hundred and fifty and three hundred thousand dollars."

The door closed behind him.

"Talk about a phony," gasped the passenger. "Did you hear what that blowhard said he lost?"

"I heard," the operator replied.

"Do you happen to know who he is?" queried the passenger.

"Yes," came the answer. "His name is Walter O'Malley."

Color drained from the passenger's face.

Charlie Dressen lasted three seasons at the helm of the Dodgers. The club performed well for him. Under his aegis, the Dodgers finished second and won two pennants. The Yankees beat them twice in the World Series. Charlie was a peppy type of go-go-go leader. A former football player, he was in the backfield of a George Halas-coached team, the old Staleys of Decatur, Illinois. As a third baseman for the Cincinnati Reds (1925-1931) he showed an almost telepathic ability in sensing a bunt.

In 1954 Dressen was replaced by Walter Alston, who had been managing Dodger minor league clubs for about nine years. He now begins his eleventh season at the helm as manager of his third World's Champions. This is a mortality far beyond life expectancy for one of today's managers. During this period Walt needed no plasma to keep the job, surviving with a strong pulse the seventh place finish of 1958 after the Dodgers moved westward. Friction at that time did not prevail and loose talk that Smokey Alston was through came from a 3,000-mile-away source: New York City. Many New York sports scribes would enjoy nothing better than to have a giant fissure appear in Chavez Ravine from an accompanying earthquake and swallow O'Malley and his stadium.

Later I will touch upon this attitude of our loyal Ebbets Field press.

With the exception of the 1958 season, the Dodgers have orbited under the guidance of Alston. Speaking of orbiting, through the years we have had two conscientious objectors to flying travel: one was Junior Gilliam while Rickey was in command; the other ground-lover, Don Newcombe, giant right-hand pitcher, after O'Malley took over.

Gilliam was playing for Alston when he was managing Montreal. The Montreal Royals were finishing up their spring training at Vero Beach and were preparing to fly to Newport News, Virginia, to play an exhibition game on their return trip to Canada. Ball clubs were just starting to be airlifted around the country and the idea displeased Junior.

Alston appealed to me for help with his problem. I told him that when he held his team meeting tomorrow

I would come over and have a little chat with Junior and square away the problem.

Cornering Gilliam, I said, "Junior, I understand you have some objections to flying."

He nodded.

"What did you do last winter?" I questioned.

"I played ball in Puerto Rico," he said.

"Oh?" I questioned. "How did you get there? There's no bridge, no railroad."

"I flew, Mr. Thompson," he admitted.

"Well," I said, after due deliberation, "I think the only decision that we can make is that if you can fly to Puerto Rico for Junior Gilliam to make a buck, I think you'll have to fly to Newport News for Mr. Rickey."

He flew—and I am very pleased for we would have been in bad shape without the great efforts of Gilliam since that occasion.

With big Don Newcombe, the problem wasn't resolved so easily. Newcombe favored train travel or any kind of travel but an airplane. I believe he would have preferred a prairie schooner or floating on a raft to rising a hundred feet off the ground. On our 1956 trip to Japan the only avenues of travel open were a boat or plane. A boat was out of the question because it took too long.

Newcombe balked, something he rarely did on the mound.

We decided it was necessary for him to make the trip. He had enjoyed a terrific year with us and the Japanese fans were anxious and clamoring to see Newk in action. Don decided to visit a hypnotist. Whether this man actually hypnotized him and personally put him aboard, or taught him the art of self-hypnosis, I never learned. All

I know was that Newk was on the plane when it took off and he flew all over the Japanese islands with us.

After O'Malley assumed charge of the Dodgers, the sign we live under—the dollar sign—which had vanished faster than the buffalo under Rickey, raised its beautiful head ubiquitously. The players, the coaches, the manager, and the front office began receiving adequate salaries commensurate with their abilities.

It has been demonstrated countless times that O'Malley has a heart that is enlarged in its generosity. After Alvin Dark's 1962 Giants rushed by the faltering Dodgers, nosing them out for the pennant, there was somberness and gloom cloaking the Dodger offices. The entire staff spoke in whispers and the falling of a sheet of paper—particularly if it contained a box score of one of the losses—reverberated thunderously. A mortuary never had it so quiet.

O'Malley chased away some of the gloom by flying more than forty of his personnel to watch the first game in San Francisco against the Yanks, and about the same number rode in the Dodgers' private plane to see the second game of the series that should have seen the Dodgers battling the Yankees. Aboard, sandwiches and refreshments were served and special buses transported the guests to and from Candlestick Park.

One of O'Malley's loves besides baseball and food is poker. Several times I have peeked over his shoulder, watching his tactics when playing with a group of newsmen. At one of these sessions I noted that he held a winning hand but folded it and wouldn't call as his opponent delightedly raked in the pile of chips.

Later I asked my boss about it, knowing he was never one to be bluffed out of anything.

He smiled and said, mentioning the name of the news-paperman, "That boy's on a very low salary."

Once when our plane landed in Las Vegas we had several secretaries along. Before we went into town where the gaming tables are inescapable, O'Malley handed each of the girls a twenty dollar bill to gamble with in the event they got the urge.

It has always been an O'Malley custom, while training at Vero Beach, to help keep office employees, press, etc. "from going stir crazy," as he put it. To avoid such a condition he would load up the Dodger Electra for trips to Puerto Rico, Havana (before Castro), Jamaica, Key West, or Nassau for a change of scenery far removed from the noises of the diamond.

It was at Nassau that I saw a sight I shall never forget. We were riding down the main and crowded thorough-fare—on the wrong side of the street, which happens to be the right side in Nassau—when O'Malley sighted the Bishop of Nassau alighting from a car on the opposite side of the street, preparatory to crossing it.

"Stop the car!" he ordered his chauffeur.

Scrambling out, O'Malley pushed his portly figure through the teeming traffic, meeting the Bishop in the middle of the street. Oblivious to automobiles and bi-cycles, the Dodger boss knelt on the pavement and kissed the Bishop's ring.

One fall, after a particularly trying season, O'Malley and his wife, Katherine, Buzzie Bavasi with his wife, Evie, and Peg and I took a trip to Honolulu. Henry Kaiser, the industrialist, telephoned and invited the en-tire group out to dinner. The ladies in our party spent a large portion of the afternoon at the beauty parlor in preparation. Unknown to them, O'Malley rented two jeeps, explaining, "We'll go Hawaiian."

Seeing our mode of transportation, the women ran for babushkas to shield their hair, and we took off, with only the vaguest idea where Henry Kaiser lived, wandering up semi-lighted streets, becoming hopelessly lost. Sighting a parked car, O'Malley leaned from the Jeep and hailed the occupant.

"Sir, is this the road to Maui?"

"I beg your pardon," replied the man.

O'Malley repeated the question.

"Sir," the man said, "I suggest that you return to your hotel and consult your travel agent."

While we knew the location of every franchise in the National and American Leagues, our geography out in the Pacific was a trifle faulty and we overlooked the fact that Maui was another island, about 225 miles from Honolulu.

O'Malley made frequent trips to Havana to watch Dodger organization players who participated in Cuban winter ball. Here a very personable man, Roberto Maduro, was active in the ownership of one of the Island clubs and entertained the Dodger brass lavishly.

With the coming into power of Fidel Castro, a gradual confiscation of the Maduro family enterprises began. At first the dictator merely nibbled at the Maduro holdings. Then he took larger and larger bites and finally distributed their plantations to the peasants.

Maduro, a proud man, was nearly bankrupt when he and his family embarked for the United States. Because of his friendship and remembering past kindnesses of this exile, O'Malley placed Bob Maduro on the Dodger payroll at a monthly salary of $1,000 for nearly two years until Maduro could become established in his adopted country.

Also escaping the tentacles of the Cuban dictator to seek asylum in the United States was Suzanne Racine, daughter-in-law of my former Montreal Royals boss, Hector Racine.

One of the mainstays of the Dodgers was Roy Campanella. Campy, in civilian clothes, was an innocuous, chunky-looking guy. Soft-spoken and gentle, he was the sort who could be imagined catching a housefly and freeing it rather than swatting it. When he slipped into his baseball armor behind home plate he underwent a quick personality change. His arm became a rifle and his movements those of a cat. He was the Rembrandt of the pick-off artists and woe to the base runner who strayed too far off base. A believer in the efficacy of prayer, he must have made converts of numerous pitchers around the circuit with his home run blasts. No Dodger was more popular or witty than Campy, and even after the crippling accident that finished his career, his rare sense of humor flowed on.

Two of our outfielders, Carl Furillo and Sandy Amoros, didn't make our 1956 barnstorming trip to Japan. This made it possible for Gino Cimoli to play regularly over there—something he didn't do all season as he was a defensive replacement for Amoros.

In Japan, Gino complained because he was playing too much. Campy buttonholed him one day, delivering a short lecture: "You should be happy to just be on the Dodger roster collecting all them Series checks every few years and always gettin' a little extra for finishin' second or third. Look at Eddie Miksis, Gene Hermanski, Dick Whitman, and Tommy Brown that used to be with us.

They kept complainin' about not playin' and they finally got traded. Now, after a year or so in the big leagues, they're in the minors."

Campy closed his little dissertation by saying, "You know, Gino, if you ain't playin', they can't find out how lousy you is."

After Campy's accident O'Malley kept him on the payroll as a scout and following the benefit game at the Coliseum for the injured player between the Dodgers and the Yankees, O'Malley, the lawyer, helped straighten out his finances.

At a staff luncheon discussion in Brooklyn involving the nationality of our fans, it was agreed that the Jewish people supported the club so well that we should hire more of them to balance our personnel in the organization. We did have Allan Roth, our excellent official statistician, several in the ticket office and in various capacities around the ball park, but few in the front office.

A week later O'Malley announced he was making Lee Scott, a former Brooklyn sportswriter, the club's road secretary. Scott pitched into his job with enthusiasm. Then one Wednesday in March he came into O'Malley's office for a meeting.

O'Malley centered his gaze on Scott's forehead. "What's that smear you have there, Lee?"

Scott began wiping his forehead with a handkerchief, explaining, "Oh, those are ashes. I just came from church."

Scott disclosed that he was of Italian extraction, had shortened his name from Scotto and was now just another one of the Catholic members of our organization.

O'Malley did not stint but bolstered our fine farm

system and poured additional monies into the Vero Beach training grounds, realizing the twin necessity of both to keep a ball club competitive year after year in a very tough league.

We were pretty happy until the day we made our annual inspection of Ebbets Field, constructed in 1913. The steel girders supporting the stands were badly rusted and corroded. Something was going to have to be done about reinforcing them. O'Malley lived in daily fear that the city would condemn the upper stand as being unsafe. Ebbets Field was small, with its 30,000 seating capacity, and the thought of losing half of that was frightening. At that time, if any person had predicted that we were going to desert the park and move 3,000 miles, we would have testified to his insanity at a lunacy hearing.

But, in reality, he could have been declared the seer of the century.

CHAPTER 8

DODGERTOWN, U.S.A.

We call it the Spring Capital of the baseball world: Dodgertown. The location is the east coast of Florida, thirty-five miles south of Cape Kennedy, formerly Cape Canaveral, four miles from Vero Beach. Here, at the Dodger Training Base, is a complete baseball college offering academic and refresher courses under Dean Walter Alston and a professorial staff which includes Leo Durocher, Pete Reiser, Joe Becker, Greg Mulleavy, Al Campanis, Andy High, Clay Bryant, Red Adams, Tom La Sorda, and John Carey, along with our minor league managers.

The seminar begins February 24th and runs until graduation day on April 25th.

The campus is spacious, consisting of some 110 acres, and was formerly a Naval Air Training Station, deactivated in 1946. The base has been occupied by the Dodgers and its affiliated minor league clubs since 1948. Two barracks serve as residential quarters: one houses the minor league ballplayers, the other—formerly the Bachelor Officers' Quarters—is inhabited by the major league players, club officials, visiting dignitaries, and the news-papermen.

Under their bylines the stories are wired in from our own Western Union headquarters by Paul Zimmerman, Frank Finch, and Sid Ziff of the *Los Angeles Times;* George Davis and Bob Hunter of the *Los Angeles Herald-Examiner;* Hank Hollingsworth and George Lederer of the *Long Beach Independent;* Phil Collier of the *San Diego Union;* Joe Hendrickson of the *Pasadena Independent;* and Bud Tucker and Bob Baker of the *San Gabriel Valley Tribune.* Thousands upon thousands of words, all datelined Vero Beach, bring huge amounts of free publicity to this resort community.

I can't assay the writing skills of the East Coast versus the West Coast, but I can say that when these members of the press file a story, it is credited to them.

It wasn't always this way.

In 1947 Burt Shotton was serving as an interim manager for Leo Durocher, who was under suspension for alleged association with gamblers in Havana, Cuba. Shotton, a quiet, imperturbable gentleman, was interviewed many times by Dick Young of the *New York Daily News.* Upon reaching New York, these spring training camp stories would appear in a column under the byline of Jimmy Powers, a featured columnist of the *Daily News.* They informed his readers that Powers was lolling around the swimming pool, fishing, and playing golf with Shotton.

Burt was flabbergasted as he read these stories. He had never spoken to Powers, much less socialized with him. After the season opened and Shotton was finally introduced to Powers, he said bluntly, "Well, I'm pleased to meet the man with whom I reportedly spent so many pleasant hours in Florida."

The focal point of our training grounds is Holman Stadium, a concrete structure equipped with lights for night baseball, seating 5,200. Here the big team—the Dodgers—plays exhibition games against the Yankees, Braves, Tigers, Athletics, and other clubs training in Florida. This attractive little stadium was built by the Dodgers without cost to the City of Vero Beach. In addition, there are five other complete diamonds and a special diamond with no outfield. The latter is used for infield practice, sacrifice offense and defense, breaking up the double steal, practicing the execution of the double play, pitchers covering first base, and any other phase of play not requiring an outfield.

Every player is given a thorough medical examination upon his arrival in camp, covering the eyes, throat, kidneys, lungs, heart, and a blood test. A Negro pitcher who had some difficulty passing his physical examination was sent home. The physical had little bearing on his release. He had some age on him and it was felt that he couldn't help one of our higher classification clubs.

Jackie Robinson questioned our decision.

"Was he sent home," Jackie asked, "because of his physical examination?"

I explained, "The physical examination had nothing to do with his dismissal."

He looked at me doubtfully.

"Jackie," I said, "we sent five white boys home last week and PeeWee Reese didn't raise any objections."

Before a player may be unconditionally released and sent away from the camp there must be a unanimous opinion among the staff of more than thirty that the youngster doesn't have a future in professional baseball. One man's dissenting vote can keep the player in camp for a further look.

On one area of the grounds are eight automatic pitching machines regulated and fed by employees from 9:00 A.M. until 4:00 P.M. One throws only curve balls and sinkers for players to practice hitting these two difficult pitches. Facing this example of the age of automation, bunting is practiced and the right- and left-hand hitters learn to hit to the opposite fields. Maybe next season we'll have mechanical batters and we'll be able to dispense entirely with the ballplayers.

Also, there are two sawdust sliding pits where a player's pants get dirty but his thighs remain unskinned. Two other areas are devoted to baselines only and on these ninety-foot paths are practiced rundown plays or pickle plays (where men are picked off bases). We try to perfect this play with a minimum number of throws because the more times the infielders throw the ball, the more chances for a miscue, either a wild throw or hitting the baserunner.

Another area is set aside as the pitching area which is known as the "strings." Here are two pitching mounds with home plates the regulation distance away. Over each home plate are crossed strings marking the strike zone. Pitching coaches take the young pitchers as well as the veteran major-leaguers to this area to work on their control.

The recreational facilities are varied. Lake Gowanus is stocked with fish for angling. Also available are: a swimming pool, table tennis, pitch and putt golf course, horseshoe pitching, badminton, shuffleboard, pool tables, and, of course, a television set. About four times a week movies of the caliber of the late, late shows on TV are run, but at an earlier hour. The camp has a canteen where soft drinks, toiletries, newspapers, magazines, and souvenirs are available.

Some players never leave the grounds during their entire stay, so complete is Dodgertown.

Vero Beach is a city of churches and each Sunday morning buses are run into town to take the players to the house of worship of their choice.

In the neighborhood of 235 players, along with eight minor league managers and about fifteen scouts, come to our camp. In past years when there were more minor leagues, we had as many as 600 players at Dodgertown. Among the thrills for the rookies who finally reach major league status is to be contacted by a representative of the Hillerich and Bradsby people in Louisville, Kentucky, manufacturers of the famous Louisville Slugger bats. The company obtains signatures of individual players and burns them into their bats—indicating that the players have arrived. For this honor the player is sent either a small stipend or a set of their fine golf clubs.

I received a beautiful matched set of these clubs as a rookie in the National League and a few years later, when I married, the Hillerich and Bradsby Company were kind enough to ship an additional set to my wife. She wasn't a golfing addict and had only swung a few clubs on a driving range and a few war clubs at me—but she was, nevertheless, very pleased with the gift. One evening we had some friends over and Peg proudly passed the golf clubs around the room.

A guest asked her, "Where did these come from?"

"Oh, there's a sporting house in Louisville that puts Fresco's name on their bats," she naïvely explained.

I quickly corrected her.

The major-domos of our outdoor classrooms circulate around the different fields, microscopically checking on the various players. They carry charts fastened to clipboards for keeping track of proficiencies, deficiencies, and aptitudes as the managers put the players through their paces.

Our players come from thirty-nine different states, three Canadian provinces, Cuba, Mexico, Puerto Rico, the Dominican Republic, Panama, and Venezuela. Many hold college degrees, but in baseball education is not of primary importance and the wangling of higher salaries calls for only native shrewdness.

Dizzy Dean is an example of the successful uneducated player. The first year he began broadcasting baseball games for the St. Louis Cardinals letters poured in to Sam Breadon, the Cardinals owner, and to Branch Rickey, general manager, from various educators, objecting strenuously to Dizzy's grammar and the influence it wielded upon the school children of Missouri and Southern Illinois.

Dean had players "sludding into third" and "going out to their respectable positions" and constantly used "ain't."

A newspaperman approached Diz for a comment on the letters.

"I notice," said Diz, "that a lot of people that ain't sayin' 'ain't' ain't eatin'."

Staff meetings are held about four times a week, at which the staff discusses each player in camp—his strength, his weakness, corrective measures, and even a switch of positions.

Three times weekly the minor leaguers gather, right after breakfast, in Holman Stadium to listen to a lecture on some phase of baseball: pitching by Clay Bryant, former Cub right-hander; outfield play delineated by Pete Reiser, former Dodger great; baserunning instructions from Maury (104 stolen bases) Wills; hitting by Andy High, former National League infielder.

All managers are continually reminded that they mustn't criticize a youngster's mistakes without immediately explaining why they were wrong and giving correctional methods. It isn't enough to tell a youngster that he strikes out too much—he knows that as well as the manager. What he must be told is how to reduce his number of strikeouts. We are in accord on what and how we teach, so that when a player leaves Dodgertown and reports to one of our managers, he can be assured that nothing contrary to what he has learned at Dodgertown will be taught.

The managers in the Dodger organization are not selected because of reputations as established baseball players. They qualified by their ability to transmit the knowledge that they have acquired through years of experience to others. They have been with us for from ten to twenty years, some as players, some as coaches or scouts. Last year we made Jim Williams manager of our Santa Barbara club in the California League. He'd been with us as a player on various affiliated clubs for seventeen years. Almost without exception our managers are selected from within our own organization because they are generally well trained in "The Dodger Way to Play Baseball."

Most of the youngsters obey us unquestioningly. They come to Dodgertown to learn. They want to learn. I remember one boy, though, who was inclined to dog it a little—he didn't always play at top speed. There was a thin curtain of doubt in his mind that it paid to hustle all the time.

Pete Reiser raised the curtain.

The rookie had read and heard of the exploits of Reiser during his playing days—how he plowed into fences in pursuit of fly balls and was carried off the field unconscious on two separate occasions.

The youngster asked Reiser: "Mr. Reiser, do you think you might have played in the major leagues a few years longer if you hadn't played so hard?"

Reiser replied, "Son, if I hadn't played so hard I might never have reached the majors."

That's the spirit we try to infuse in all Dodger players.

The first three weeks of the training camp are operated solely for the major leaguers as they strive to get in shape for the exhibition games and the long season that lies ahead. Our dining room facilities are set up as in a hotel. Waitresses handle individual tables. The menu is varied, affording choices of appetizers, soups, entrees, salads, and desserts.

There's a waitress who still works our dining room who hasn't recovered from the time Frank Howard couldn't make up his mind what to order after a strenuous day on the practice field, and said to her: "Bring me the entire menu."

Frank is not a switch hitter, but observers agree that he could, with little effort, become an ambidextrous eater.

O'Malley has often said of Howard, "I'd rather clothe him than feed him."

When the minor leaguers descend upon Dodgertown, our population suddenly booms. The entire Los Angeles Dodger office personnel, with the exception of the Accounting Department and the ticket office, transfers to Vero Beach. The Accounting Department is busy paying the bills run up at spring training and the ticket office is busy selling tickets to finance the huge Dodger operation.

With the influx of the minor leaguers, we discontinue our individual table service and revert to a cafeteria-style dining room. It would be impossible to serve the many players and administrative personnel a regular a la carte menu. The dining room opens at 5:30 P.M. for supper and a half hour earlier the line begins forming. Some of these hungry youths are anxious to bolt their food and rush to downtown Vero Beach to take up their positions on the various corners and whistle as the girls go by.

Democracy operates at its finest when the dining room doors swing open. The rawest rookie may head the line and Sandy Koufax be wedged into fifteenth position. Even Mr. and Mrs. O'Malley are often seen far back in the line, awaiting their turn at the steam tables. It is not at all unusual to see a young, aspiring Negro ballplayer drop into a seat alongside a member of the Dodger varsity who happens to be from a southern state. Never has there been, in our sixteen years at Vero Beach, an incident involving racial discrimination.

Often as many as eleven games are played on the campus of this baseball college morning, afternoon and night. Approximately 200 practice games are held at

Dodgertown during the course of the camp. An amazed newspaperman once said, "This is the only training camp I've ever attended where I could miss half the day's workout and still see a doubleheader."

One of the main advantages of a central training camp is fraternization. The players of all clubs become acquainted with one another; firm friendships develop. During the season if a player should be transferred from one club to another, or when the Dodgers cut down to their active limit of twenty-five, he goes to a club where he is not a stranger to the players or the manager. Because of this no orientation period is needed for adjustment to a different club.

We must keep in mind that these players come to us as third basemen or outfielders simply because some college, high school, or American Legion coach told them they were meant for these positions. Perhaps the coach had two excellent third basemen and, deciding that he wanted to keep both in the lineup, sent the other to the outfield. So we will change the position of some players. We learn that here is a boy who is a real good hitter, has a fine pair of hands, but runs too slowly to become a major league outfielder. If such is the case we might try to make him a catcher or a first baseman, where running speed is not so important. It might take hours of coaching but we feel it is worthwhile to place him in a position where we can squeeze the most from the physical equipment he possesses.

Ofttimes Leo Durocher is thought to be rough on rookies, but any advice or caustic remark he growls at them generally penetrates. Noticing a rookie infielder limping around, Leo inquired, "Son, what's the matter?"

"Coach, I've got a sore heel," I heard the rookie say. "Hurts me when I try to run."

"Don't worry, Son," Leo advised, "it's probably just from the lead in your fanny that fell on your heel."

One of the strictest rules appears on a sign hung over the entrance to our dining room:

CHILDREN UNDER 16 YEARS OF AGE ARE
NOT PERMITTED IN THIS DINING ROOM.

Our reason for this is not because we fear that Frank Howard in his hungriest mood might reach for a child. Every major-league club that has as many players as we have in a central location fears epidemics of children's diseases. Many of our players have not had mumps, measles, chicken pox, whooping cough, etc., and we must safeguard them from infection. This necessitates the players who come to Vero Beach with their families taking apartments, motel rooms, and small rented houses with other families. For living off the base they receive a subsistence.

The boys may tire of the coaches' perpetual cries of "hustle. . . . hustle" but no advice could be better. I recall one of my first games in the majors. It was against the Giants, a team that had been my childhood idol. I was playing with the Pittsburgh Pirates. Toward the tail end of the 1925 season I was suddenly inserted into the lineup when our second baseman, Johnny Rawlings, broke his leg sliding into second.

Ross Young, of the Giants, one of baseball's greatest hustlers, was on first base with one out. A ground ball was hit to Glenn Wright, our shortstop. Glenn flipped the ball to me as I covered second.

Before I could pivot and make my throw to first, something hit me!

My first thought was that the first base stand had collapsed onto the field. I wound up six feet to the outfield side of second base, flat on my back. From this supine position I gazed up at Young with a pained expression, mumbling, "Kind of a rough way to treat a youngster, wasn't it?"

Ross looked down at me scornfully. "Well, Son, you know we aren't playing for marbles."

It was just such a jarring contact with a splendid competitive athlete early in my career that forcibly and painfully brought home the realization that we *weren't* playing for marbles; for I learned in a few seconds that what I had formerly considered just a game was really a serious business. I had chosen baseball as my profession and with it must come a change of attitude and outlook. It was a far cry from trying to win a varsity letter at Columbia University.

Young's remark taught me an important lesson—namely, with my limited ability I could become an asset to my club by showing a real bear-down hustling attitude.

To convince our baseball hopefuls of this necessity is not an easy task.

Before the start of spring training, all of the minor-league players must be signed to contracts with their respective clubs. On our Spokane and Albuquerque clubs each general manager signs its own players. We allow this because they are veterans of many years' experience in negotiating contracts.

However, in our lower classifications the general managers are less experienced and since their charges are young ballplayers, we prefer to handle their contract negotiations from the Los Angeles headquarters. Just the wrong reply to a young ballplayer during his negotiations can create a morale problem that might be difficult to untangle.

There are always a few so-called holdouts. The minor leaguers are arguing in hundreds of dollars, the major leaguers in thousands. Nevertheless, their arguments are just as sincere. The fellow who hits well and fields spottily avoids mentioning his lackluster performance in the field and, instead, concentrates on his hitting prowess only. Pitchers who don't notch many victories but possibly have a good earned run record, will relate how poor fielding teams stole games from them or the rough infield accounted for lost games they otherwise would have won. Some players don't even mention hitting or fielding averages in their efforts to get a few more dollars. They use the hardship approach: their wives are expecting babies and that means more mouths to feed.

We explain to this group that it is impossible for us to place all married men on the high-salaried Dodgers and distribute the single men throughout our minor league clubs. Performance has to be our principal yardstick and the number of children sired by the player may swell his ego but is of secondary consideration.

This may seem heartless. It isn't. We aren't running a philanthropic organization. Baseball is a business. Though minor league clubs draw poorly, the thinking trend of its players is, "Well, the Dodgers can afford it—they drew two and a half million fans last year." Chances are most of these youngsters will never play a game for the parent Dodgers.

Yes, the Dodgers can afford it, but the overall picture is distorted. At Salem, Oregon, for example, one thousand spectators is a terrific gate. What we netted in Los Angeles is partly siphoned off in the subsidization of Salem and our other minor league affiliates. We still must operate as economically as possible.

Players argue that they can't make both ends meet on what they're making in the five months they play. Of course, no restrictions are imposed on seeking other jobs in the winter to supplement their baseball earnings; but these boys who have been playing for five, six, or seven hundred dollars per month want to continue living well during the summer and still have enough left over to attend college or have extended honeymoons during the winter.

It's a desirable trait in a boy to wish to complete his college education, but is there a valid reason for the Dodgers to foot the bill? Or to pay for his new car or to make the down payment on his home? I was in the majors—at least with the Phillies—for two years before I owned an automobile that would start on a cold morning. Maybe that's why my legs were always in good condition. Youngsters today expect to begin just where Daddy is at present, forgetting that he worked for twenty-five or thirty years to reach his station in life. To work only six months a year and compete with a parent is simply at variance with the facts of life.

Bavasi, while he believes a player's contract to be a personal matter, is of the opinion that the public has a right to know what their heroes are making. The Dodger payroll last year averaged around $22,000 per man. The major league minimum is $7,000.

How are salaries determined?

"Four factors," Bavasi said. "One, ability. Two, length of service. Three, drawing power. Four, size of park."

The Dodgers depart from Vero Beach well in advance of the minor leaguers, whose seasons open later. Before leaving, Alston impresses upon the remaining managers the importance of continuing instruction even into the playing season—to keep the players practicing on cut-off plays, base stealing, and particularly bunting. Bunting, it appears, has become a lost art in these days of the home run. Everyone plays for the big inning and managers hate to sacrifice an out in the hopes of getting just one run. Major leaguers are, on the whole, poor bunters.

Players want to unload every time with the big swing and hit the ball on the "money end" of the bat, as they call it. The only fair territory the average major-league hitter sees today is in the lap of some customer sitting in the bleachers. There are few Willie Keelers who try "to hit 'em where they ain't." A baseball adage often heard is, "Hit home runs and you'll drive a Cadillac; hit singles and drive a Chevy."

Carefully as we may drill the boys, some are apt to miss steal signs or other signs. A missed steal sign can cost your club a game—possibly a pennant. Even veterans can forget them.

Last year the Dodgers were playing the Mets when a funny thing happened—and Casey Stengel had nothing to do with it. Should the steal sign be flashed to a base runner on first, it is the job of the first base coach to give another sign to the runner to be certain that he has the sign. Alston had briefed his players at a pre-game meeting that if the first base coach called the runner's last name that meant the steal was on.

Frank Howard was on first base with the count 3 and 2 on the hitter and Alston wanted Howard to be off and running on the next pitch. It was Pete Reiser's job, coaching at first base, to alert Howard. Frank had played for Pete at Green Bay, Wisconsin, and Victoria, Texas.

"Be careful now, Howard. . . . heads up, Howard. . . . one out, Howard," Reiser kept signaling.

The batter twice fouled off the pitch but Howard seemed glued to the bag. Pete repeated the signals.

At length Frank turned toward Pete and said, "Come on now, Pete, you know me too well to call me by my last name."

Reiser, changing systems by running through our old steal signs, managed to get the message through.

After the season opens, in order to keep a close tab on our scattered players, the various managers are required to send daily reports of their games to the Los Angeles office. Reports contain the weather, attendance, average attendance and how it compares with last year. To this form is attached a box score of the game. Below, on the same page, a space is reserved for comments on the game, from the manager, which are not obvious from the box score.

A box score can be like an inaccurate map leading to a buried treasure. If we in the office examine a simple box score and note that one player got three hits in four times at bat and another went hitless, we could be deceived. The no-hit fellow may have hung out three line drives or outfielders made circus catches on him; and the apparent slugger-in-the-box score might not reach the fence if all his hits were laid end to end. He could have beat out a bunt or blooped a couple of broken-bat singles over the infield.

The truth may be concealed in a box score that shows that the pitcher was jerked in the fifth when the opposition scored four runs. What it fails to disclose is that the second baseman bobbled an easy grounder, spoiling a routine double play that would have closed out the fifth inning without any runs and allowed the pitcher to finish the game. These are the points that the managers are required to clear up in their comments.

Managers also tender health reports, advising us of any injuries on their squads and reporting on how previously injured players are progressing. A manager might indicate that a certain player on his team is having difficulty in that classification and his recommendation is that he be sent to a lower one where he can hold his head above water and regain his old confidence.

One of my pet annoyances when I managed New Orleans was this detailed report I had to make for the parent Brooklyn club. Branch Rickey, as I previously explained, disliked generalities, demanding specifics. So I sent the following on a young pitcher: "This boy is wild low. He doesn't have enough stuff to be wild high."

We prefer having a player in a classification too low for his ability rather than in one too high. Self-confidence is a tremendous asset in a player and one they all start with. It is our job to see that this trait is not taken out of him. If he, through lack of experience, can't cope with certain types of pitching or the pitcher with certain types of hitters, a spoilage can result—or at least a delay in his arrival in the big leagues.

Many of the boys have come to us as stars from high school or college. In spring training they find themselves on a club with an entire constellation of stars. Now they, as individuals, don't twinkle so brightly. Some flounder for a while, taking long to become established. If we place them in leagues where they feel like take-charge guys, instead of letting the league take charge of them, their hopes never dip.

To be a whale in a fish bowl is better than a minnow in a lake is our credo.

It was only a few years ago that practically every major league team had at least one graduate of Dodgertown on its roster. With the decline in the number of leagues and the resultant reduction in the number of players in the Dodger organization, this is no longer true. There are, however, still more graduates of Dodgertown in the major leagues than from any other camp. The list includes such players as Roberto Clemente, Don Demeter, Chico Fernandez, Don Hoak, Gino Cimoli, Elroy Face, Bob Aspromonte, Carl Warwick, Roger Craig, Bobby Lillis, John Klippstein, and others.

In college or high school our trainees may have been outstanding students of languages, German or, perhaps, Greek. Such lingual skills are wasted at Vero Beach. Here the fledglings run smack against an argot that cannot be taught . . . only picked up by ear. The expressions are unique and voluminous, and a compilation could compete in size with an abbreviated standard dictionary. They are pure slang related to baseball.

Here is a smattering of the diamond dialect:

ALIBI IKE: Player who has an excuse for every mistake
ALL-AMERICAN OUT: A poor hitter
ANGELS (not the ball club): Clouds in the sky that make it easier to judge fly balls
ANNIE OAKLEY: Intentional base on balls
BANJO HIT: A ball hit on end of the bat for a hit
BARBER: Very talkative player
BASEBALL SADIE: Gal whose weakness is ballplayers

BEAR'S NEST: A poor hotel

BLAZER ... HUMMER ... POWDER RIVER ... THE EXPRESS: The good fast ball

BLEEDER: A lucky or fluke base hit

BLIND TOM: Umpire

BLOOPER: Pop fly dropping behind the infield

BLUE-DARTER: Line drive hit

BOILER: Stomach

BOLSHEVIK: Clubhouse lawyer

BOOT ... FLUB: An error

BUSHES ... STICKS: The minor leagues

BUTTERFINGERS: Infielder who makes many errors

CAN OF CORN: High, lazy fly to the outfield

COUNTY FAIR ... BUSHER: One who doesn't behave like a professional

COUSIN: A batter's favorite pitcher

CRIPPLE: Two balls and no strikes and three balls and no strikes pitches

CROOKED ARM ... PORT-SIDER ... SOUTHPAW: Left-hand pitcher

CUNNY THUMB: Pitcher who throws a lot of slow stuff

DEAD FISH ... NOTHIN' BALL ... LOCAL: A slow pitch

DICK SMITH: A player who travels alone

DOG IT: Not doing your best

DOWNER: Good overhand curve

DUCKS ON THE POND: Runners on the bases

DUSTER ... BEAN BALL ... GILLETTE PITCH: Pitch thrown near the batter to loosen him up

FLAKEY: A player who acts a bit odd

FROZEN ROPE: A line drive base hit

GET TWO: Try to make the double play

GLOVE MAN: Good fielder

GOOSE EGGS: Scoreless innings on the scoreboard

140

GOT BIG ONE LEFT: Batter has two strikes on him

HASSOCKS . . . CUSHIONS: The bases

HIGH HARD ONE: Good high fast ball

HIGH SCHOOL HOP: A big high bounce, easy to field

HIT THE DIRT: Slide into a base

HOMER: Umpire who appears to favor the home team

HORSE COLLAR: A hitless day with 3 or 4 at bat and no hits

HOSE: The throwing arm

HUSTLE BUMPS: Marks and bruises on a player's body

IN THE WELL: Fly ball hit to a sure outfielder

JAKER: Player consistently out of lineup with real and imaginary ailments

JOCKEY: Player who cleverly rides the opposition

JOHNSON AND JOHNSON: Player who always has adhesive tape showing

LEG-HITTER: Batter with no power who beats out infield hits

LONG MAN: Relief pitcher expected to go five or six innings

LONG STRIKE: Long hard-hit ball that goes foul

LOW BRIDGE THE HITTER: Brush hitter away from the plate

MONEYBAGS: Big bonus player

MONKEY SUIT: The baseball suit

MORNING GLORY: Rookie who starts well and fades

NIGHT CAP: Second game of doubleheader

OPEN THE DOOR: To make an error and prolong an inning

PIANOLA . . . LAUGHER: An easy victory

PINK SLIP: Unconditional release

PLATTER . . . DISH: The home plate

PRO: One who plays and conducts himself as a major leaguer should

PUBLIC ENEMY #1 . . . OPTICAL ILLUSION: The curve ball

PUTTY: Player prone to injury

PUTTY ARM: Weak throwing arm

RABBIT EARS: Player who hears everything said by the fans and opposition

RHUBARB: Ruckus with the umpires

RIBBIES: Runs batted in or R.B.I.'s

ROCK: A stupid or bonehead play

ROCK PILE: Rough infield

SALARY DRIVE: A player's hustle last month of the season

SCATTER ARM: Infielder who makes inaccurate throws

SHORT MAN: Relief pitcher who goes from one to three innings

SHOTGUN: Strong accurate arm

SHOWBOAT: A player who never catches a ball with two hands that he can catch with one

SIEVE INFIELD: Poor defensive infield

SKIP THE DEW: To run exceptionally well

SNAKE . . . DOWNER . . . FISH HOOK: A real good curve ball

SNAKE-BIT: Unlucky

SQUEAKER: A very close game

SQUEEZE THE PITCHER: Umpire refusing to call the corner pitches

STOPPER: Effective pitcher who prevents losing streaks

SUNDAY PITCH: A pitcher's most effective pitch

TAKE A NAP: Get caught off first base

TAPE MEASURE JOB: Very long home run

THE APPLE: What bothers a poor competitor in a crisis

THE BOOK: Information on the strength and weaknesses of other clubs

THOMAS EDISON: Pitcher who continually experiments with new pitches

TO CADILLAC: Taking it easy running the bases

TOE HOLD: Batter digging in at home plate

TOOLS: A player's talents

TOOLS OF IGNORANCE: Catcher's equipment
TOURIST: Player who performs on several teams
TWIN-BILL: A doubleheader
UNDRESS SOMEBODY: Hit the ball real hard
WASTE ONE: Deliberately throw a ball out of the strike zone
WET ONE: Illegal spitball
WHEELS: A player's legs

CHAPTER 9

WESTWARD HO!

It wasn't just one girder rotting on Ebbets Field—it was all of them.

Nothing in our world is indestructible, including steel. The girders needed support, if not replacement, and a hundred and one other refurbishments were necessary. Yearly maintenance on Ebbets Field was mounting, running to astronomical figures of from two hundred and fifty to three hundred thousand dollars annually.

We needed a new ball park. Badly. But was it a prudent investment to build one in Brooklyn?

The last thing Walter O'Malley wanted to do was to leave Brooklyn. But a fear haunted him—fear that Brooklyn was becoming a decadent borough. Facts stood out sharply:

No sizable building had been constructed with private funds in Brooklyn since 1927. New buildings of any magnitude, such as courthouses, jails, or Hall of Records had been financed with city funds. The Del Webb, Zeckendorf, Tishman, Frank Lloyd Wright, Luckman, and Pereira architectural face liftings that were changing the appearance of many cities were noticeably absent in Brooklyn.

Brooklyn reminded me of an expanded William Bendix face waiting to be beautified by plastic surgery, with no doctor willing to operate.

When I first played in Brooklyn as a member of the Dodgers there were four department stores of ample size, housing class merchandise. Only one remained in 1957. Newspaper Guild trouble had caused the closing of the *Brooklyn Eagle,* the last of four local newspapers. The loyal and substantial fan, the family man, had moved away. He was now living in Westchester County, out on Long Island, in New Jersey, or in Akron, Ohio.

He was replaced by the undesirables.

I brand no race, color, or creed as objectionable. They all have their scum. But, unfortunately, the scum was now thick in Brooklyn. The element drifting into decaying Ebbets Field and using unprintable language in catcalling to the players or in the stands would shame women to the extent that on Ladies' Day only a handful of the most rugged and probably deafest of the distaff side could weather the sting of words.

Ebbets Field had a double-decked grandstand, and to sit safely in the lower portion it was almost necessary to wear raincoats on a day when the sun was shining brightest. Rowdies cascaded beer, ice cream, peanut shells, etc. onto the heads and clothing of those seated below. Cash boxes were repeatedly stolen from public telephones. Urinals were even pried from the men's lavatories and carried home, for what purpose no one could guess.

O'Malley held many conferences with Captain Emil Praeger, of Praeger-Kavanagh-Waterbury, New York architects, who was Chief of Design for the Navy and instrumental in the design and construction of the Triborough Bridge and other notable structures. There was hardly a drawer in O'Malley's office that did not contain the plans for a beautiful park on some prospective site in Kings County.

He was happy and anxious to construct a new baseball park.

The question was WHERE?

One of the sets of plans dealt with a site in the City Hall Plaza which was being reconstructed by the Borough of Brooklyn but later taken over by the Red Cross. Then, another in Fort Green Park, located fairly near downtown Brooklyn; but in order to acquire this site a seldom used two-block-long street needed condemning.

The city refused to bless this.

Another site seriously considered was at Flatbush and Atlantic Avenues over what is the Brooklyn Terminal of the Long Island Rail Road. To carry this out meant condemning a small portion of the produce market from which various merchants had wanted to vacate for years because it was outmoded, unsanitary, and rodent-infested.

Plans were drawn for a park here but the city wanted to include a bridge spanning Flatbush Avenue and a multiplicity of other improvements, eventually to cost the city approximately eighty million dollars.

Robert Moses, New York City Commissioner of Parks, showed O'Malley sites scattered around the city. His favorite had the waters of Flushing Bay on one side and a cemetery on the other.

O'Malley threw up his hands in a hopeless gesture.

"I can't draw from the cemetery and few people will swim the Bay to see games."

I told him, "Some of the language used by the fans

wouldn't be fit for even the dead to hear if we build there."

In our Ebbets Field location there were close to 400,000 people within walking distance, in addition to two subway lines, bus lines, and half a dozen trolley car lines feeding us—yet they would continue to supply us with the same element of people, a pretty indigestible potpourri, at best.

Commissioner Moses came up with still another site, Flushing Meadows, where the present Shea Stadium, home of the Mets, was recently completed. For years engineers had tried in vain to build a six-inch road through that area, but it kept sinking, as it was being built on filled-in land reclaimed from Flushing Bay.

O'Malley, because of an engineering background acquired in college, knew it would cost in excess of three million dollars for support pilings before the stadium concrete could be poured. True enough, contractors had difficulties in certain areas of the Mets park that sank faster than Casey Stengel's ball club has the past two years.

Visualizing building a triple-deck grandstand erected on the meadows, O'Malley believed it too risky. "By the Fourth of July," he speculated, "maybe I'd have only two decks above ground and by Labor Day a single deck visible."

O'Malley was a third generation New Yorker. He had his roots here but he didn't want them under water.

To this I'd add that we'd have to stop dealing with Wilson Sporting Goods, transferring our business to some firm selling skin-diving equipment.

During these ball-park-searching days, O'Malley often repeated the statement, "I want no politicians for landlords."

He wanted to build a park himself with his own plans and his own funds. After the experience of the Giants in San Francisco, I can well understand these desires. Candlestick Park squats in a cold, windy, foggy spot where offensive odors creep into the area from low tides—not always from the Giant pitching. Even now the Giants and the politicos are at loggerheads over who shall paint the seats and what steps can be taken to alleviate the sinking of the parking areas. They never know when a Volkswagen might disappear.

Those are some of the things that O'Malley wished to avoid.

Talk became rife of moving the ball club out of Brooklyn.

Then the complaint mail began arriving. An average of 100 letters daily reached the office from Dodger fans berating O'Malley for even considering such a move. Strangely, the familiar Brooklyn postmark was missing on the letters. Seventy per cent of these letters came from such faraway places as Oklahoma City, Nashville, Omaha, and the like, where ex-Dodger fans had settled.

These were not people who could be counted upon as regular patrons of the Dodgers. They were comparable to the noted subway alumni of Notre Dame—always fans but never spectators.

Bavasi, Red Patterson, Dodger Publicity Director, and I faithfully answered every letter. Our answers followed a pattern:

We can tell from the postmark that you left Brooklyn, apparently to do better financially and improve living conditions for your family; and we feel the Dodgers certainly have this same right to move wherever they wish.

148

In New York a villainous image was being projected of O'Malley. He was characterized as a traitor, selling out his birthright, and castigated as a Benedict Arnold. The image-creators were the New York sportswriters and wire-service boys. They feared losing a way of life—namely, freeloading. Should the gravy train be derailed, their plushy assignments were finished. The day of cakes and ale was over.

With the Giants, Yankees, and Dodgers playing in the Metropolitan area, each newspaper assigned three and sometimes four sportswriters to the baseball beat, in addition to some of the columnists. These gentlemen of the press spent four to six weeks in Florida during spring training, escaping the rigors of northern winter, generally at the expense of the ball clubs. Food, lodging, cigars, and liquor to which they were unaccustomed were furnished. They traveled luxury class on the speediest jets, were quartered at swank hotels.

Now suddenly the rug was threatening to be jerked out from under them and in its place many of these same writers would have to cover high school contests, West-chester County dog shows and rodeos, and ride the crowded subways to reach these stirring assignments. Some of these writers were syndicated nationally, and the venom poured from their typewriters, spattering over Walter O'Malley.

They accused him of putting a ring in Horace Stone-ham's nose and leading him to the greener pastures of California. Anyone acquainted with Mr. Stoneham will attest that none can lead him anywhere he doesn't care to go—and few can follow him places where he wants to go. Stoneham's decision to evacuate was the result of the scant 600,000 paid admissions to the Polo Grounds during his final year at that park. It was Minneapolis or San Francisco, O'Malley or no O'Malley.

O'Malley, the press slurred, was "money-grabbing, selfish, unappreciative. . . . a man who was letting down the loyal fans of Brooklyn."

I'd like to refute these charges by asking a few simple questions: Manufacturing companies move. . . . perhaps to a state where they get a tax break, raw material is handier, shipping costs less. Why not a baseball team?

In a nation of free enterprise, is it wrong to wish to improve yourself?

These same sportswriters who were belaboring O'Malley had come to New York from Connecticut, Oklahoma, and Pennsylvania—obviously to better themselves with the large New York dailies.

New York bigwigs, among them Governor Averell Harriman and Mayor Robert Wagner, were offering special inducements, setting up committees and signing legislation to study property condemnation and bond issuance for a new Brooklyn ball park. Desperate attempts were being made to keep the team from moving. Should O'Malley have attempted to drive out of town, it wouldn't have surprised me to find roadblocks stopping him.

On February 1, 1957, O'Malley purchased the Los Angeles franchise in the Pacific Coast League, together with Wrigley Field, Los Angeles home of the Angels, for $3,000,000. The move alerted the Los Angeles City Council. Through the years the Council had made feeble efforts to secure the Washington Senators' and the St. Louis Browns' franchise. These were more or less feelers and the hands stretching out to do the feeling contained no money in their fingers.

We were in spring training at Vero Beach in 1957

when Los Angeles city officials descended on us like a plague of locusts—with one difference: this was a honey-bearing variety. Among the group were Mayor Norris Poulson; County Supervisor Kenneth Hahn; President John Gibson of the City Council; Councilwoman Rosalind Wyman; Councilman Ernie Debs; Sam Leask, Jr., City Administrative Officer; and Milton Arthur, Chairman of the County Park and Recreation Commission.

They came down laden with all manner of colossal, gigantic, spectacular, and other Hollywood adjectives in their promises. The group convened with the Dodger brass at Bud Holman's ranch, covering several thousand acres, some thirty miles from Vero Beach. Holman was a Dodger director.

Somehow the connotation of the words "colossal," "gigantic," and "spectacular" seemed dwarfed in the middle of this expanse of land. Yet, such a vast territory and its seclusion were necessary, for had they convened at Dodgertown, Vero Beach, New York sportswriters would have been provided with an opportunity for the biggest massacre since Custer's.

When the Far Western delegation learned, in the course of the discussions, that O'Malley wanted to build his own ball park with his own funds, there was a mass quivering of joy. Handsprings were in order, except for Councilwoman Wyman, as such acrobatics would not have been considered dignified in mixed company.

They spoke glowingly of Chavez Ravine: 600 acres, owned by the city, to be made available as a park, with access roads and parking facilities. This, as time went on, dwindled to 300-odd acres—and most of the acreage was odd, to say the least.

Chavez Ravine sounded to me like a Western movie

location. Maybe I was confused by a name such as Bloody Gulch. Still, perhaps I wasn't far wrong. Blood was almost spilled in the Ravine before work on Dodger Stadium started a few years later.

On May 1st O'Malley came to Los Angeles, and one of the first things he did was to plop into a cab and tell the driver, "Chavez Ravine." Walter had not as yet seen the proposed site of the ball park.

The driver scratched his head. "Chavez Ravine?" he repeated dumbly.

"Yes, yes," O'Malley said impatiently. "How long have you lived here?"

"Five years."

"And you don't know where Chavez Ravine is?"

"I always thought it was a Mexican prize fighter," the driver said, opening a map.

The first time I saw Chavez Ravine was in the company of Captain Praeger. I immediately thought of Hades without the River Styx. The topography featured a series of crisscrossing gullies, all trying to escape each other. I couldn't visualize any game being played there except tag by the gophers.

"There isn't a spot level enough for a game of tiddledy-winks," I gasped to Captain Praeger. "How in the world can we ever build a ball park here?"

"You'd be surprised," the expert said knowingly.

I simply couldn't conceive, at first glance, the moving of eight million cubic yards of dirt.

Only sparse habitation was visible. Scattered here and there among the barren, dusty ridges were dilapidated shacks. There was an attractive school building on the acreage but this had closed for lack of pupils. I could understand why. The weather-beaten remains of a church were losing the battle of survival to erosion, causing one to think that God had abandoned hopes here.

I asked what kind of taxes the residents paid and I received the answer, "Very little. Most of them are squatters."

It developed that the city didn't even have title to 300 of the original 600 acres dangled in front of O'Malley. About nine parcels of land owned by private individuals and appraised at $80,000 were right in the heart of the area. This land had to be purchased because we couldn't have the players running through a tavern on the way from first to second, or have Duke Snider sit on someone's front porch while playing center field.

To accomplish this purchase seemed, at this time, relatively a matter of formality. Little did we know what was in store for us.

Within a few years Chavez Ravine—dusty, arid, unused —was to be transformed, in the eyes of the obstructionists, into a Garden of Eden below whose lush surface flowed a river of oil worth millions. Yes, and even deposits of cobalt and uranium.

Historians were on the verge of rewriting California history books. Balboa was no longer the exploratory hero who discovered the Pacific Ocean, but a wandering bum who should be given hell for overlooking Chavez Ravine.

Some of the skeptics were suspicious of O'Malley and his intentions. Here was O'Malley, the city slicker, come to take advantage of an unsuspecting public. He would probably get title to all of this land and build a pre-fabricated plywood ball park which he would use for a couple of years. He would then sell the land to some corporation on which to build a nut and bolt factory. I do not know what the need is in Southern California for bolts, but I can assure you the other commodity is in good supply.

Amidst much fanfare, pomp, and ceremony, the Dodgers came to Los Angeles to open the 1958 season. The hundreds of towns and communities comprising the Leviathan of the West Coast went wild. Citizens thumped citizens solidly on the backs, proclaiming:

"We're now officially the sports capital of the U.S.A."

There was a parade and everywhere hung signs: WELCOME DODGERS.

But behind those banners of goodwill, using hit-and-run tactics, lurked the opposition, an evanescent, tough, powerful adversary; retreating, counterattacking, remaining nameless, never identifiable.

O'Malley began tilting with ghosts. Because of his ancestry, he enjoyed a good clean brawl.

"I don't mind fighting somebody," he told me. "As a matter of fact, I relish a good tussle. However, I want to see whom I am fighting. I feel as though I'm in one of those battle royals where they blindfold everybody and eight fighters in the ring start swinging. You don't know whether you're hitting friend or foe."

Before dwelling at length on the Battle of Chavez Ravine, the sniping at the Dodgers, and the thrusts and forays at them by bands of invisibles, I want to touch on two problems that immediately became evident:

We had a poor team.

We had no place to play.

It was necessary for us to have an aging, below par ball club our first year in Los Angeles. Let me explain this mystifying statement. If we had remained in Brooklyn for the season of 1958, a rebuilding process would have started in which we would have inserted youngsters into the lineup to replace a number of veterans that we felt were over the hill. We couldn't do this now. We had to revamp our plans and delay our rebuilding program. We were invited to another city to become the Los Angeles Dodgers, and the organization strongly felt the inadvisability of juggling the team around at this time.

The fans in Los Angeles and throughout Southern California were led to believe that the Brooklyn Dodgers were coming here and we could not break faith with them and field a team studded with unknown newcomers from the Montreal and St. Paul clubs. Everywhere I went where men talked sports I'd hear:

"Isn't it great?!—Erskine, Newcombe, Reese, Furillo, Hodges, Snider—players we've heard about for years will be playing right here in our own back yard."

Although these players were not, by any stretch of the mind, through, they were reaching the twilight of their careers. We had to bring a team with some identity into this new territory: the veterans whose names rolled off tongues when the Dodgers were mentioned. Unfortunately, Roy Campanella could not be among them as he had suffered the car injury that left him paralyzed. I have always regretted that our faithful Angeleno fans never saw this superb athlete perform.

It would have been strange indeed if we moved westward with unknowns playing positions occupied by the old guard. Instead of yelling for a double play, some might have cried "doublecross."

As a result of what we believed was sacrificial fairness on our part, the team finished seventh. This is the only time I can recall since being associated with the organization that we ended in the second division, out of reach of pennant honors. This tailspin of the Dodgers was fuel for the fires of hatred that burned in the typewriters of former Dodger sportswriters back east. They made the most of it.

Surprisingly enough, with a few replacements here and there and the addition of Wally Moon from the Cardinals, the team bounced back to tie with the Milwaukee Braves in 1959 and then defeat them two straight in a thrilling play-off.

From there we went on to overcome the speedy Chicago White Sox four games out of six for the World's Championship. This, to my knowledge, was the only time in baseball history that a team climbed from the lowly position of seventh one year to achieve such honors the next season.

Walt Alston will claim that a team effort won the pennant in 1959. Others argue that the fine pitching of Drysdale, Craig, Podres, and reliefer Larry Sherry was the tower of strength bringing us home in front. I think Gino Cimoli, who wasn't even with the team, was responsible.

There was a day in 1958 that the Dodgers were using a certain sign for the squeeze play in order to alert the third base runner that the play was on. Nothing is more embarrassing to a manager and his team than to get what we call half a squeeze play. In other words, have the batter receive the sign and bunt the ball and the runner remains at third, unaware of the play. Or the man on third comes charging toward home and the hitter takes the pitch because he missed the sign. They try to protect as much as possible by being certain that everybody is enlightened.

On this day the alert sign for the man on third was the use of his last name. Ordinarily with a runner on base, the coach would say, "Alright now, Jack. . . . be careful. . . . be careful, Jack," and suddenly the coach says, "Look out, Smith"—and the play is now on.

Cimoli slid into third as an alert photographer snapped a picture of a close play. Hodges was at bat with Charley Dressen coaching at third. Right after Cimoli dusted off his trousers and stood on the bag, the photographer called to Dressen:

"Who's the fellow who just slid into third?"

Dressen walked several steps toward the photographer and whispered, "Cimoli."

Gino sort of turned around, not quite sure he heard his last name mentioned, but since Dressen didn't repeat "Cimoli," he assumed the play wasn't on.

But the photographer hadn't heard Dressen clearly and he again asked the name of the runner who slid into third. He was persistent. A picture without identification is worthless.

Dressen had returned to the coaching box and, somewhat annoyed over the interruptions, yelled, "Cimoli."

Now Cimoli was sure the play was on.

He streaked for home as the pitcher was finishing his delivery. Hodges saw Cimoli out of the corner of his eye, started to swing, but held up. Gil was puzzled as he hadn't seen any steal or squeeze sign. Should Hodges have swung —as only Gil could—he might have decapitated Cimoli and driven Gino's noggin over the short left field fence as he slid into home plate.

An injury to Cimoli and we couldn't have made the trade for Wally Moon with the St. Louis Cardinals. If we hadn't made the trade, it's highly doubtful that we could have won the 1959 pennant. Moon furnished the spark that carried what had been a complacent ball club to the pennant and World's Championship.

The future success of our team was hanging by a single

thread as Cimoli sped toward home plate that night in 1958.

When O'Malley was granted permission to move the Brooklyn Dodgers to Los Angeles, Horace Stoneham had the blessing of the National League to move his franchise to Minneapolis.

O'Malley wanted the New York Giants to come to California with him. The National League did not. O'Malley then made it clear that he didn't want to move to California unless the same privilege was granted to the New York Giants.

The Giants and the Dodgers, enemies on the field, were like a married couple who stick together through the years despite feudings. O'Malley recognized this natural rivalry would continue with the Giants in northern California and the Dodgers in the southern part of the state. The distance was greater than it had been back east, but the feeling between the two cities was, if anything, stronger. Each city would enjoy scoring a triumph of any kind over the other.

The way was opened for Stoneham to go to the West Coast. It was up to O'Malley to convince him that California should be his choice.

Stoneham advised the Dodger president that he had a ready-made ball park in Minneapolis but had no notion of what kind of a park he would get in the Golden Gate city or what type lease the city fathers would tender him.

O'Malley contacted Mayor George Christopher of San Francisco, who agreed to fly to New York and confer with Stoneham and O'Malley. The three men met in the Lexington Hotel, where Christopher guaranteed Stoneham that his city would construct a modern ball park for the Giants.

"What kind of a lease will the Giants have?" Stoneham queried.

The Mayor admitted that he was not acquainted with ball park leases, inquiring of O'Malley what would be considered a fair lease for both parties.

O'Malley extracted his fountain pen and wrote a proposed lease on the back of an old envelope.

Mayor Christopher scanned O'Malley's notes, passing them to Stoneham. They both agreed that this would be a fair lease.

Thus, in approximately thirty minutes, Walter O'Malley was able to do for Horace Stoneham and his Giants what was going to take him years to accomplish in Los Angeles for his own Dodgers.

A mountainous barrier that, at first, seemed unscalable blocked the Dodgers in Los Angeles: where to play. 22,000-seat Wrigley Field was inadequate, the Rose Bowl in Pasadena not feasible. Only the Los Angeles Memorial Coliseum remained. The Coliseum—reconstructed with additional rows added—really came of age for the 1932 Olympic Games. Football found a home there—105,306 fans jamming the place for the Notre Dame-Southern California contest of 1947. Since that time the Coliseum has housed such diversified events as basketball, fireworks displays, political rallies, tennis, ice shows, music festivals, pontifical masses, ski shows, Easter services, midget auto races, boxing exhibitions, a long Billy Graham crusade, and BASEBALL.

The latter was the most difficult to stage.

For the privilege of playing our national game in the Coliseum, O'Malley paid dearly to this tax free project.

To put it crudely but accurately, the Coliseum Commission had the Dodger President over a barrel and paying through the nose. We had no parking revenue, concessions being limited to the sale of scorecards and souvenirs. Since this was a Memorial Coliseum, the sale of beer was prohibited. The amber fluid is a great source of revenue to all ball clubs. Especially to the Dodgers. Gussie Busch, the brewing king from St. Louis, told Walter O'Malley that Dodger Stadium is the biggest saloon in the U.S., selling more beer annually than any single place dispensing liquor. This destroys the theory that beer is primarily a hot weather drink, as most of our games are played under the lights in the cool of the evening.

We were to play in a ball park with only one front row and a deck of high rise seats which went into orbit. The last, or 79th, row was altitudinous enough to train an astronaut. The way the baseball field was laid out in the Coliseum, it was a weak pitch shot over the left field fence and three dollars in a taxicab to the right field barrier. Widening of individual seats and installation of a new press box trimmed the seating capacity to 93,000.

Pete Rozelle, present Commissioner of the National Football League, and then General Manager of the Los Angeles Rams, objected to our diamond plans. Pete wanted the infield located at what is known as the peristyle end—the exact opposite to the end we desired.

"The football players will have difficulty playing on the skin or dirt part of the infield," was Rozelle's contention.

What short memories these mortals have.

Pete has forgotten that without the assistance of major league clubs there might not be a National Football League. Chances are they would still be playing in smaller cities. All the early games in the NFL and most of the present ones are held on baseball fields and the skin area is part of the gridiron. Among these are Yankee Stadium, Polo Grounds, Pittsburgh, St. Louis, Cleveland, Baltimore, Philadelphia, and Chicago. Chicago, Pittsburgh, St. Louis, and Philadelphia are owned outright by the baseball clubs and not by municipalities. Pro football would have rough sledding without those cities.

For the teams the Rams unveiled during our occupancy of the Coliseum, it mattered little what they played on. To actually help their stuttering forces they needed a field slanting downhill every time they gained possession of the football.

Hundreds of thousands of dollars were paid by the Dodgers for Coliseum rental, and a good portion of these funds was used to build the Los Angeles Sports Arena, a truly beautiful edifice.

The Coliseum was an inferior classroom for our growing fans to familiarize themselves with big league baseball. Players seemed swallowed up and lost in the immensity of the stadium. In left field a screen hung along the front of the stands. It originated from the foul line. The distance was ridiculously short. To homer in right field, the ball had to clear a six foot wire fence, which at times deepened to 440 feet—a measurement sounding the death knell for slugger Duke Snider.

The Coliseum is even a poor place for football, let alone baseball. Only 28,300 seats are between the goal lines. If you buy a ticket from a speculator on a crowded day, this enthusiastic scalper always assures you that it's a choice seat on the fifty yard line. And if you should actually be on this coveted marker, the distance from your seat to the field can be so great that a 300 pound linesman such as Roosevelt Grier is reduced to a flyspeck.

Baseball fans had trouble getting oriented. Perspectives were off. On routine fly balls they rose and cheered in expectation of them clearing the fences. It was as odd as playing a game of cricket on the streets of Harlem.

The Dodgers nonetheless drew tremendously—five million fans watched our team the first two years in the Coliseum. The first World Series ever played on the Pacific Coast saw over 92,000 fans on three successive days crammed into the Coliseum.

As I said, no alcoholic beverages are sold in the Coliseum. This failed to halt the pleasures of the thirsty. The local law was as difficult to enforce as Prohibition. Empty bottles were in evidence all over the stands at the conclusion of the game.

"Beer and baseball go together like meat and potatoes," a rabid fan told me. "No one is going to prevent me from bringing a six-pack into the Coliseum."

No one ever did.

The fans screamed, cheered, blew "charge calls" on bugles under the broiling sun to help the battling Dodgers dominate. The ubiquitous Larry Sherry turned in four super-relief stints. When the Series ended, he kept up the torrid pace on the banquet circuit. Any place where the sound of cutlery rang out loud and clear, our Larry was seated as the honored guest.

CHAPTER 10

THE BUSINESS OF BASEBALL

SAN DIEGO—Would your heart stand the pulse-stirring excitement of seeing a baseball trade announced before your very eyes?

"Would your doctor permit you to court the high blood pressure thrills of seeing a third-base coach signed? How could you keep calm while watching the Spokane Indians getting their schedule approved? Could you stand the suspense of seeing two sporting goods houses dicker for a year's contract on windbreakers?

"Do you enjoy seeing a hundred unemployed men jockeying for less than fifty jobs? Like to see two hundred newsmen competing for a story that could be inscribed on the head of a pin, with room left over for a wall motto?

"Then the winter baseball meetings are just the ticket for you. More fun than watching clocks run."

This is the way Jim Murray of the *Los Angeles Times* began a column called MAD, MAD BASEBALL on the minor league portion of the 1963 winter meetings held

163

in San Diego, the major league portion continuing in Los Angeles.

Each year around the first week in December the minor leagues and the two major leagues hold a convention. It bears no resemblance to an American Legion convention. Your wife will even help you pack to get to this one. The minor league part is generally held in some far-flung place like Miami, Tampa, Rochester, or San Diego, as in 1963. The majors generally convene in major league cities or not far distant.

Conventions should, of course, be held in some central location, easily accessible to all minor league clubs. Money wasted on transportation by these lower-class minor league clubs could be used to help keep the leagues operating. Their mortality rate is at an all-time high.

Baseball people convene to pass legislation under which they will operate for the coming year. The legislation, without fail, is resolved into a contest between the haves and the have-nots. The latter arrive with hats in hand, tears in eyes, campaigning for legislation that will even up the strength of clubs in the major leagues.

Instead of clubs building up to the Yankees, White Sox, Dodgers, Giants, etc., efforts are made to bring about by legislation the lowering of the caliber of baseball down to the level of play of second division clubs.

Completely overlooked is the fact that as long as athletic contests have been held, there are winners and losers. Neither the National nor the American League has ever experienced an eight club tie; and now with ten clubs in each league, the possibility of all clubs being even at the end of the season is more remote.

No business restricts itself in the acquisition of new talent as much as professional baseball. The handcuffs bind our wrists and the keys have been thrown away. We can't sign players until they graduate from high school. If they graduate from high school and still have American Legion eligibility, we can't sign them until the national finals of that organization are completed in September.

Until quite recently college players could be signed at any time. First we agreed to wait until the close of the Frosh year; but then legislation reared its head, restraining us to signing only juniors and seniors. Collegians can leave college and go to work for Sears Roebuck or General Electric, or join the Peace Corps at the drop of a book during their undergraduate days. If they choose professional baseball for a career, they are required to wait until the final exams of their Sophomore year.

What is termed a selection period is also held during the minor league convention. This is a means of advancing players to higher clubs than the clubs on which the original signing club feels that they can play. The selection or draft of contracts was originally set up for the purpose of enabling players to advance in their profession. This rule was instituted to protect players in the minors so that if the club holding title to their contract did not believe they could play in a certain classification, other clubs or organizations could select the contracts for a nominal consideration.

Thus they would be afforded an opportunity to play as high as their ability warranted—at least the drafting club hoped this would take place. Perhaps the drafted outfielder hit only .220 in Tacoma, but the selecting club believes their managers or scouts are geniuses who can convince the hitter that the curve or low-sinker is his best friend and he can become a .300 hitter. The pitcher who has a burning fast ball but fewer curves than a woman with a fencepost figure is selected and hopes that some managerial Svengali will mumble a magic incantation and lo, he has a wider assortment of curves than Jayne Mansfield.

In recent years the drafting of players has lost its original intent, purpose, meaning. A ridiculous and socialistic "first-year player" rule was enacted, in an attempt to save the major league organizations from themselves in committing financial suicide by giving fuzzy-cheeked high school boys, who are farther removed from the major leagues than the moon shot, fantastic bonuses to sign contracts. The monies doled out on bonuses to free-agent players was reaching astronomical figures and becoming a thorn in the side of the clubs.

This rule was intended to curtail such extravagance. It did just that. But also it was the reason for clubs signing approximately 300 fewer players each year the rule has been in effect. Who is there to say that among the 300 unsigned players directed to other fields of endeavor there wasn't another Koufax or Mantle?

Clubs may now sign from 30 to 100 free-agent players at any bonus they wish and the sky is the limit. A club would be foolish to sign several players at ridiculously high bonuses when sound baseball practice dictates that only a couple could be protected from the clutching claws of the opposition. The only way an organization can protect these youngsters is to place them on the roster of the parent club. Numbers do not matter. Install as many of these players of one year's experience on your major league club as you wish. The catch is that only one of these so-called protected players may be optioned out to the minors. The remainder must stay on the active list and compete with Hank Aaron, Mickey Mantle, Willie

Mays, Roger Maris, and others. They must also hit against the likes of Koufax, Drysdale, Ford, and Marichal. It's simple to guess how competitive a team might be with five or six of these embryos on its active list.

They would probably finish in the now extinct Piedmont League.

What of the other fine young prospects whom an organization has signed?

Since it's obvious that a club designed to compete for a pennant in its respective league can have only one or two of its players protected, the others are put up for grabs for an $8,000 fee at the draft meeting.

This is a real "scavenger hunt" by the less industrious and the less adventurous clubs who hope to steal a future DiMaggio or Bob Feller for eight grand. These first-year players eligible for selection are not the culls left over after the signing club protected all of its good players. These are the fourth, fifth, and sixth best youngsters that the organization inked.

A club could lose ten or fifteen of its better prospects. This could easily mean that its full year of scouting was down the drain. The drafting club can option off all of the players it drafted from other clubs, but only one player brought to the parent club from within its own organization may be optioned.

It becomes a "You draft my ballplayers and I draft yours" sort of game. If we wanted your players badly enough we would have made a stronger pitch for them during the original negotiations.

Since all first-year players are draftable at the termination of that initial year, clubs dispatch these youngsters in the spring with a fervent prayer that they have lousy years; that they'll be overlooked in the winter draft that can blow an ill wind. Managers become the accomplices, the middlemen, surreptitiously hiding their capabilities. They are played under difficult conditions. If he is a left-hand hitter, he performs against left-hand pitchers. If he is a left-hand pitcher, he's in there pitching against right-hand hitting teams. The policy is: do anything to make him unattractive to visiting scouts.

Some clubs put the youngsters on and off various inactive lists purposely to bench them. A club may have twenty-five players on the field with numbers on the backs of only twenty. The others are masked marvels, numberless to protect their identity from the eyes of the scavenging scouts.

This game of "hide-and-see-the-player" is a cloak-and-dagger maneuver that only needs trenchcoats and foreign accents to make it acceptable TV fare.

The chicanery can easily delay the young ballplayer in his efforts to climb to the top, and cost him one full year of an all-too-short career.

Another important phase of the convention—sometimes pitifully futile and sad—is the efforts of the unemployed to make a new connection. These are the field managers who were fired because the front offices failed to provide them with satisfactory clubs. Others include managers sacked because their center fielder, a .350 hitter at mid-season, broke his leg sliding into a base and his club went into a tailspin because his replacement didn't know which end of the bat was up. Still another manager may receive his walking papers because last year's 20-game winner got a sore arm in spring training that wouldn't let him comb his own hair, much less toe the mound during the regular season.

The job seekers are easily recognizable. Their eyes are

darting around searching for hope—hope in the person of a prospective employer. Most of their faces show the effects of sun drenching. Unlike sportsmen exposed to the outdoors, their tan is not the healthy brush-painted kind, but what might be called a worried weather exposure. The coloring is etched into the crags, crevices, and furrows lining their faces—and the cracks widen as a forced smile overspreads their features.

While their walk is not identical, it is a reminder of the walk to the mound for a meeting with the pitcher in trouble. Now it is the ex-managers who are in trouble.

Joined in the lobby with them are front office personnel who never pitched an inning or had one time at bat, but have been separated from their jobs because the fans failed to patronize a seventh-place club; or it snowed the first ten days of the season, preventing spectators from attending their games.

There are probably five field managers to every administrative man searching for a job, and all know the baseball facts of life: there are fewer than twenty minor leagues now, versus a post-war high of more than fifty. None of these men are johnny-come-latelys. They've been in baseball from fifteen to forty years.

For some reason, this small but determined army of the unemployed seems to congregate in the rooms of the sporting goods exhibitors—the manufacturers who have uniforms, bats, etc. for sale. These are known as "Hospitality Rooms" where expectant purchasers of their equipment are entertained. Here the price of the drinks is within the price range of everybody—they're free.

None of these merchants has a job to offer in which he could take advantage of the excellent backgrounds of the unemployed. Men coming to these rooms to hire managerial or front office help are nonexistent—yet the job seekers sit in these quarters by the hour. They commiserate with each other on the pitfalls of managing, blasting the fellows responsible for firing them. They talk about how lucky so-and-so was to get such-and-such a job. After consuming all the drinks they can't hold, they weave out into the lobby, and the same eyes—but now not nearly as clear as they were—keep searching.

They are the sad men of the convention, mostly out of work because of some factor over which they had no control, whether it be injuries to key players, incompetent material, lack of cooperation from the front office, or a passing of the buck to the low man on the totem pole.

Here at the convention, trades that started taking shape at the World Series are either consummated or called off completely. Managers and general managers are trying to trade a load of ashes for a load of coal. Players whom the manager has cussed and discussed suddenly become valuable property when offered to other clubs. Pitchers who didn't start the last two months of the season are spoken of as potential 20-game winners. All they need, it is alleged, is a change of scenery. Outfielders who hit a lowly .210 are in for good years and offered in trades because their marital troubles are now patched up. The player's wife never swung a bat—unless it was over his head—but she was the villain, the cause of his complete collapse at home plate.

Managers are talked into trading their third baseman for the other fellow's first baseman. You need a first baseman and he needs a third baseman, so both clubs are deliriously happy—or at least advise the press that they are. Neither club has a replacement for the fellow they traded but each club plugged a hole. They forget that they also created another hole and it makes no difference whether the hole is in the right side of the boat or the left side—the boat eventually sinks.

Sportswriters and the wire services converge on the meetings to get the "hot" stories that they expect to funnel from baseball's winter meetings. Yet, infrequently does any worthy news—few headline makers—come out of the meetings. The convention cities set up elaborate press headquarters with bulletin boards and typewriters equipped with fresh ribbons. The ribbons are all black. This is a mistake. They should have some with red.

Because that's the financial position the minors—without exception—are in.

Revealing announcements are displayed on the bulletin boards, such as: NEW YORK YANKEES ANNOUNCE RENEWAL OF WORKING AGREEMENT WITH SHELBY, NORTH CAROLINA, OF THE WESTERN CAROLINAS LEAGUE; or JOE BLOW NAMED TO MANAGE KEOKUK OF THE MIDWEST LEAGUE.

When no important announcements or trades are made and the liquor threatens to run low, the press congregates around Casey Stengel, raconteur and prophet, for some untranslatable story that will justify their flying from Boston to San Diego. When the copy desk in Boston receives the Stengel story, they don't know whether to blame the mistakes on their reporter, Western Union, or Stengel himself.

Another event transpiring at the convention that receives several thousand words of second-guessing and criticism is the meeting of the Rules Committee. This is composed of a group of major and minor leaguers who annually and often semiannually consider recommendations for rule changes.

There are always suggestions to speed up the game.

They come not from the fans, but from the writers who have a deadline or a date to meet and want to hurry from the ball park. Others insist that since everyone is throwing the spitball and the rule prohibiting it can't be enforced, it should be legalized. Many clamor for a free substitution rule so hitters can hit for fielders and fielders can field for hitters.

I hold the line at changes. To me a great deal of the charm of baseball lies in the fact that the game is fundamentally and primarily the same as many years ago. If your grandfather hasn't been to a ball park in forty years, he can go see a game tomorrow and follow and understand every move. The basic plays and rules remain steadfast year in and year out.

This doesn't happen in football. Should a fan miss attending football for one season, he won't know who is eligible to receive a pass, how substitutions are made, or what happens when the kicking team touches a punt inside the ten yard line. A woman can at least pretend to understand baseball, but not football. Few women grasp it, and some coaches don't either, for that matter.

Minor changes we have made—such as bringing gloves off the field after an inning, or the elimination of a freak oversize catching glove—can bring a storm of criticism from the press and club officials. Self-styled progressives have labeled members of the Rules Committee "simple-minded fools" because they passed a rule eliminating a glove that has no place in a ball park simply for the reason that they have a pitcher who throws what he calls a "knuckler" and the catcher can't catch it unless he's wearing a circus tent.

What the pitcher needs isn't a bigger glove for the catcher. His delivery doesn't always get that far. What he really needs is a rule calling for smaller bats or more outfielders—some of whom could be placed strategically in various sections of the bleachers.

One grousing club owner mentions the fact that none of the Rules Committee has a nickel invested in baseball and he has five million disbursed in the game, and he asks why should this group of mere salaried employees set the rules by which his players must perform.

I am a member of the Rules Committee and it is true that I don't have any cash investment in baseball. I do, however, have forty-one years of my life bound to the game as a player, field manager, scout, farm director, and club executive. I didn't have to invest ten cents to get any one of these positions I held.

I wonder what strange set of playing rules we would have if the Rules Committee were chosen according to the amount of money each individual had plowed into the game. Would the players have to concern themselves when they came to bat with such problems as capital gains and batting averages, consolidation of the short-stops' and second basemen's batting averages, or the merger of the salaries of pitchers and catchers? And would a player hesitate to drive in the winning run in the seventh game of the World Series because the winner's share could put him in another income bracket?

Of such trivia are conventions composed.

Occasionally decisions are made at these meets that turn out to be of cardinal importance, that make pennant winners out of also-rans and great managers from unsung minor leaguers such as Joe McCarthy, Johnny Keane, and Walter Alston.

Jim Murray says, "Baseball is a complicated mansion in which the upper floors are superb, hung with tasteful tapestry and gold fixtures in the bathrooms. But the bottom floors are rotting away."

By the "bottom floors" he refers to our minor league clubs.

Maybe he's right; and perhaps some day, at one of these meetings, we'll find a way to rebuild and strengthen the "bottom floors."

CHAPTER 11

FROM OFF THE CHEST

I GUESS I'm just a lucky guy. Whenever I begin talking people listen to what I have to say. They have to. I speak at club meetings, fraternal organizations, before civic groups, and, following the luncheons or dinners, my audience is too weighed down to stagger away and escape. Now, once again, in this book, I have a captive audience. The odds are in my favor that if you spent money to buy *Every Diamond Doesn't Sparkle,* you're going to keep on reading. This gives me a chance to get a few beefs off a battle-scarred chest against which some hot grounders have bounced in the past.

I keep hearing gripes about how tough the poor major league players have it these days with the ten-team schedule necessitating a four-to-six-hour hop in air-conditioned planes. Don't waste your sympathy. They've been spared the old days' discomforts, such as a thirty-six-hour train ride from Boston to St. Louis in a tourist class pullman, with cinders drifting in the windows. A cinder in the eye felt the size of a golf ball. The train swayed and jerked along, stopping at every crossroad. A stomach seemed upside down after the first fifty miles. It made you wonder if the engineer hadn't abandoned the tracks and taken off over the fields.

If you were a rookie, it meant an upper berth, which was twenty degrees hotter. You got to St. Louis in time to play an afternoon game with the thermometer touching 106° and the Mississippi River steaming up the whole place. They call it humidity. Cut it with a knife and you can spread it on bread. Then it was off to your hotel to try to sleep. Air-conditioning hadn't been perfected, and if the room had an electric fan, all it did was circulate the hot air to be certain you didn't miss any of it. The only relief seemed to be in the bathtub, but that was temporary. When you tried to get dry, you stayed wet.

Yes, players today sure have it tough.

When I sat down with the Rules Committee in 1962 we wrote the enlarged strike zone into the regulations for 1963. I look with satisfaction on our brainchild and feel that it is good to be right for a change.

At the beginning everybody was knocking the higher strike area as a useless gimmick. I steadfastly maintained that you could speed up the game. Now games generally run from ten to thirty-five minutes faster, and a mere ten minutes saved is considered miraculous by the man in a hurry—although I've never figured out what is done with the extra time. Possibly it gives people ten minutes' time bonus in which to get themselves killed driving home after the ball game.

Hitters squawk to the high heavens, or to anyone on earth who will listen, about the big strike zone. BIG! Why, first they cut it down to the shoulders; then to the armpits. I defy any umpire to tell you where a batter's armpits are in the uniforms they wear today. Then they moved it down to the letters.

So what happens? All the clubs were putting their names down around the belly. Honestly, the strike zone had shrunk down to the place where it was tough on the pitcher and yet the batting averages of the hitters kept getting lower.

With the higher strike zone the hitters are committing themselves earlier. Some complaints have been voiced that the umpires aren't calling the high strikes consistently. I'll neither confirm nor deny this. It is unimportant whether they call them uniformly or not, or whether the pitchers throw the high strike.

The rule stands and the batter never knows when to expect the pitch will be called. So he has to swing to protect himself. It makes for sound reasoning that when pitchers throw fewer pitches in a game, the accent's on speed. This compensates for the way a lot of hurlers fiddle around on the mounds. . . . pick up the resin bag and look at the stars overhead, check the outfield or the bench, and hold conferences with the catcher that assume the importance of a United Nations meeting before they decide to throw the ball.

So, despite the meetings on the mound—which are a natural thing because man is basically a lonesome animal and anytime there's more than one of the breed around they're bound to be drawn together—the game is faster.

In 1963 the games were speedier, the batting averages sank, the pitchers' earned run averages were lower, there were fewer bases on balls and more strikeouts, so the enlarged strike zone must have had some effect since it was the only important rule change that dealt with pitching.

Now if the Rules Committee could only dream up a cure for the rash of home runs we would, of course, run the risk of becoming unpopular with the fans, but we'd certainly revert to baseball the way it should be played and keep Abner Doubleday from revolving in his grave. Baseball is a game of stolen bases, the hit and run, the squeeze play, and the sacrifice, but recently everyone just wants to play "long ball."

It's becoming too much like Russian roulette. Every hitter, 160 pounds or 200 pounds, is trying to drive the ball as far as he can and writers even attempt to measure the flight of the ball after it leaves the park. The game should get back to sliding and away from the slider. Brute strength is beginning to dominate. The crack of the bat wielded in the hands of some giant who has so many muscles there's no room for all of them on one body is a sweet symphony in the ears of the fans.

My job with the Dodgers is to supply plasma from the minor league teams to the parent club when that dread disease "second-division-itis" rears its ugly head. When taps for the Southern Association—the fourth league to fold since the 1961 season—sounded for economic reasons, a copious blood reservoir for the majors dried up.

If the present alarming trend continues, the major league club owners, farm directors, and others with a hard-cash interest in baseball will have to sit down on their thin wallets to decide how many leagues are necessary to maintain the present caliber of big league baseball. Perhaps an outright subsidy of the minor leagues is the answer. We have almost reached that now. The majors can't operate without the minors. It would be comparable to having colleges and eliminating high schools and grammar schools. There must be a training ground somewhere for the major leaguers of tomorrow.

Even subsidized village baseball teams have their financial troubles, as Milt Rayburn, publicist for Schroon Lake, New York (population 890), a resort in the Adirondack Mountains, will verify. Some years ago the Schroon Lake team was hurting at the gate because on a slope behind home plate stood a cemetery where an excellent and not-too-distant view of the game was possible. There was no grandstand, and more persons were sitting on the grave markers watching than were sitting in parked cars or along the grass sidelines.

The manager, realizing that the only revenue came from lemonade made in a private bathtub and ticket sales, called the State Troopers to oust the free sitters on the grounds of "desecration of the graves."

The police tried to comply. Two uniformed officers entered the cemetery and attempted to dislodge the occupants.

"We're visiting our relatives," they were told, "and we're sitting on their tombstones. Is there a law against it?"

The police could quote no law.

We can't afford to kid ourselves that the colleges can supply the talent necessary to keep the majors rolling. College football and basketball lure the crowds. Baseball doesn't draw enough to sell two cases of soft drinks on a hot afternoon. A gregarious person can feel like a prisoner in solitary confinement, he is so alone sitting in the grandstand. As long as the colleges are closed during sixty per cent of the baseball season, we can never reach the stage where the colleges are our farm systems as they are for pro football and pro basketball.

Only in California and the Southwest does the college player enjoy a weather advantage allowing his team often to play a 50-game schedule. In other sectors teams are lucky to squeeze in a dozen games, with rainouts, cold, and snow conditions forming against them. The fact that college baseball is a losing financial proposition means the athletic treasury is drained of X number of dollars that might be used to bring some revenue-producing fullback to the ivy-covered buildings. The debating team shows up better in the budget. All they ever lose are their voices.

Because college baseball coaches aren't exactly overpaid, it is difficult to obtain competent coaches. Some can barely teach the rules of the game or hit a decent round of infield practice. An exception is Rod Dedeaux of Southern California, recently voted the NCAA Coach of the Year for the third time. He knows baseball as well as a major league coach, and his squad—provided they had a few extra pitchers—might finish out of the cellar in a Class B league. Dedeaux has something like a dozen of his former players coaching in high schools throughout the state, and, as a result, a chain reaction has set in that produces some pretty fair ballplayers.

The talent hot spots for players are shifting. They used to be Pennsylvania and the Carolinas. Today the unpolished nuggets are mined from the Southwest and California. The highest percentage comes from California.

Much conversation revolves around the spitball today. Does he or doesn't he? This question is asked of every winning pitcher in the game today. The long finger of accusation is always pointed at someone believed to be using this illegal pitch. What does a pitcher need with a spitball? He has the fast ball, curve ball, change of pace, knuckle ball, screw ball, slider, and sinker. I say that he'd better learn how to control the pitches he now has in his repertoire or enlarge his variety. Many of the current crop of pitchers haven't the foggiest notion what a spitball is or how to throw it or what it is supposed to do. They sneak a little perspiration off their wrists or foreheads and throw what passes for a spitball. They should see a real old-fashioned spitter, saturated with tobacco juice or slippery elm, sailing toward the plate, leaving a jet stream in its wake as it jumps a foot in some unpredictable direction.

I'll never forget when I faced Burleigh Grimes for the first time in the major leagues. It was something to see him holding his hands in front of his face. He could have been one of the ten most wanted men in America and the FBI couldn't have identified him while he got the ball good and wet.

I figured that I was a smart young kid and Grimes, with his glove concealing him like a mask, was blacked out as far as the bases were concerned. It never occurred to me that in his long and successful career he had had men on third before. The first time I reached third and he started bathing the ball with tobacco juice, I took off for home plate.

He threw me out by ten feet!

As I walked to second base when the inning was over, he called, "Hey, Kid! Where do you think you're playing? Still in the bushes?"

"Yes," I replied unwisely, "I felt right at home when I saw you out there pitching."

"Okay, wise guy," he sneered. "Every time you come

up to the plate from now on, I'm gonna knock you down."

And he did just that as long as we played against each other.

Grimes had a memory like an elephant and an arm that seemed nearly the length of that animal's trunk.

The demise in the number of minor leagues cost some ballplayers their jobs. The Dodgers control more than 300 players and now, with the folding of the four leagues in the last few years, it could mean that some of the veteran players we intended taking to camp may have to be released. All decisions must be resolved in favor of the player who has a chance to help us for the next ten years and against the fellow with only a couple of years left in his legs.

There are plenty of vacancies on the rosters of our lower classification clubs, but it isn't easy to fill those clubs. With living costs spiraling, it's difficult to sign kids from $250 to $400 per month. We have to sign them to the higher classification clubs that pay bigger salaries. Now, for the first time since the Dodgers organized a farm system in the late thirties, we don't have at least one club in each classification.

We operated seven minor league clubs last year. During the boom years of late forties we have a high of twenty-eight clubs. Those were the days when a man with a tidy cash reserve could build a stadium and people would buy a ticket just to find out what was going on inside. In 1949 a total of fifty-nine minor leagues operated within the structure of organized baseball. Since that record there's been a steady and drastic shrinkage. By 1957 only twenty-nine remained. Further attrition has reduced the starting list for this season to eighteen.

We've just about reached the absolute minimum. This constant shriveling is a dangerous thing. If it increases the majors may find themselves struggling in troubled waters up to their noses. Admittedly there were far too many leagues in 1949. That was a post-war phenomenon. Everybody had money rattling around in their pockets and every town wanted a team—and usually got one. Fledglings among the organizers of these teams and leagues didn't have "baseball savvy." It was a survival of the fittest, and not many were fit.

But even now the knowledgeable operators who could franchise in populous areas find the going rougher and tougher. Radio broadcasting of major league games into minor league areas weakened the towns, and the televising of the games into minor league cities delivers the KO punch. And still some big league clubs are blithely lining up more of these game-of-the-day programs. The dying gasp of these minor league operators was "The majors are eating their young." These men must stop and try to visualize what professional baseball would be like without the minor leagues. Youngsters are not born ballplayers. They must be trained and developed from apprentices to the finished major leaguers. The only satisfactory incubators thus far have been the minor leagues.

Where would the young players come from? Where would they send the surplus talent for further seasoning? How would they expect youngsters to choose baseball for careers if there was room only for those who were good enough to start in the majors?

I've heard it said that baseball could get along completely divorced from the minor leagues by adopting professional football's system of picking up players directly from school. I've attended many of the NCAA college baseball tournaments and I would hate to take the pick of these fields and enter a Class B league with nothing else. The pro football teams get, in the college graduate, not only a developed and trained football player but a highly publicized individual. Last season we signed Jeff Torborg, a catcher from Rutgers University, the most sought-after college player in the country. When, with considerable fanfare, we announced Torborg's signing, our writers asked, "Who is he?"

The average big league club has five farm affiliates. The Dodgers have eight this year—three ownerships and six working agreements. Thus, nearly 144 minor league clubs are involved in eighteen leagues, assuming that they are all eight club setups, which they aren't. I contend we're down to bedrock with only eighteen minor leagues ready for play this season.

That's why my job—the care and feeding and hand raising of 300 little future Dodger players—is becoming harder. . . . to handpick the green rookies, hoping they'll blossom into full-bloom Dodger basebulbs.

Our gardens are disappearing.

While a newspaper may cost only ten cents to buy, in the long run that same paper may cost us thousands of dollars. The father of a prep school phenom reads that scouts are drooling over his son. Some sportswriter who has never signed a player in his life announces that the bidding will start at $35,000. That sounds like a nice round figure to the father, and that becomes his asking price for the first bid.

The second reason is the fierce competition for a young

player today. It's virtually impossible to come up with a sleeper because the extensive scouting network infrequently overlooks a boy's capabilities.

Our record in the National League has been established almost solely by products of our farm system. All but three of the present World Champion Dodgers were developed on our own minor league clubs. Exceptions are Wally Moon, Lee Walls and Bob Miller. Willie Davis, our speedy center fielder, has performed fantastically when you consider that three years ago he was playing Class C ball at Reno, Nevada. Today he's considered one of the leading outfielders in the game, plus some fine hitting.

Fans overlook fielding. Most fans check the batting averages solely, when selecting their All-Star teams. You must remember that every player wears a glove for each of the nine innings, but comes to bat only three or four times a game. This enhances the value of the glove. A poor defensive center fielder can kill a ball club, regardless of how well he hits.

Ron Fairly just has to play on our club. You can't keep a fellow like Ron out of the lineup. If Ron can't find a place in which to play for us, we've got a hell of a ball club, that's all. Ron has the advantage over some of the others in that ever since he was seven years old someone with professional experience was teaching him how to play—first his father, former minor leaguer, then Rod Dedeaux. The result was that he was several years ahead of the average rookie. While Willie Davis and Ron Fairly arrived quickly, Tommy Davis was making the grade in the normal four years. He's led the National League in batting for each of the last two years. Tommy is the first National Leaguer to repeat as the batting leader since "Stan the Man" Musial led in 1950, '51, and '52.

There is a lack of deep love for the game today from the viewpoint of the player. More and more we find our scouts adding on the scout report cards this comment: "He likes to play."

We used to take this for granted. A boy would go to sleep at night with his bat at the foot of the bed. Now if we are interested in signing a youngster the boy interviews us and so do his parents, his agent, and often the family lawyer. And bear in mind that this is in an era when baseball players make larger salaries, have a tremendous pension plan, travel more comfortably, and eat better than ever before.

Maybe this is the new age of living.

One of my serious beefs is the minor league fans in different cities where we operate baseball clubs.

We must bear in mind that one of the principal assets essential to a young ballplayer is his confidence. Shake this, and his ability can quickly dissipate. We signed him because he was a standout in high school or college and has great faith in himself. His thinking is irrevocably bound to optimism. He believes devoutly that he has a chance to become a good player.

Then he is sent to some baseball town many miles from his home city, his friends, and perhaps his girl. Invariably there is a bumptious fan sitting in the grandstand—the village comedian or wit—who visualizes himself as a combination of Bob Hope-Jonathan Winters-Milton Berle. He entertains (?) all fans within listening range by riding certain players to the point of digging his verbal spurs in deeply.

For a slight miscue, he may trumpet: "Why don't you go to bed earlier at night?" Or, "You must have had one too many last night."

The fan forgets ballplayers have the same problems as do those sitting in the stands. They walk the floor with the baby when it has the colic. They worry over finances. They ponder about the health of their parents back home. They have marital misunderstandings that they are trying to thrash out. These are often contributing factors to a player's performance on the field.

Every ballplayer knows that the morning after the game a box score is going to appear in the newspaper, showing the number of times he went to bat, assists, errors, etc.—a record of his successes and his failures.

I wonder how this same self-styled comedian of a heckling fan would feel if the morning paper ran a box score of his efforts, successes, and failures of the previous day. If this were the case, I am sure he would be more sympathetic towards the youngster trying to establish himself as a professional ballplayer.

There is the group of fans who feel that because they have paid a dollar and a half to enter the park, it's a carte blanche invitation to insult the players. Ballplayers have a name for these merciless riders: "Wolves." Some towns are worse than others in the number of "wolves" but almost every town has at least one. Many towns show consideration for the sensitivity of the athletes and give tremendous hands to the players whether home or visiting team members.

If the fans in the minor league stands would remember that these boys playing for their cities are apprentices going through a learning period, they might be easier on them. An exhibition of patience and some word of encouragement or applause for the youngster when he performs creditably or makes a supreme effort, instead of a blast of sulphurous language, could be the difference between keeping his spirit alive or breaking it altogether.

Following a meeting of the Rules Committee in San Diego, at which the use of the oversized catcher's glove was banned, I picked up a paper and saw that Charles Finley of the Kansas City Athletics had said, and I quote: "The members of the Rules Committee are a bunch of simple-minded fools."

I understand that this statement has since been denied by Mr. Finley but since I had seen a reappearance of these quotes, I felt his accusation called for some statement of defense, even though I was busy on the convention floor, unable to attend the Rules Committee meeting which did outlaw the glove. I waited for Charley Segar, the chairman of the Rules Committee, to make some statement, but none was forthcoming, so I decided to answer Mr. Finley myself.

The oversized glove was used by the catchers on certain clubs that had knuckle ball pitchers. Those catchers have found it extremely difficult to handle the knuckle ball with the standard-size glove. However, I recall two pint-sized catchers from the bygone days—Ray Schalk of the Chicago White Sox and Muddy Ruel of the Washington Senators, later traded to the Detroit Tigers—who caught spitballs, shine balls, emery balls, coffee-bean balls, and mud balls with a glove that's even smaller than the regular one used today—besides sometimes catching hell from their managers. I hate to think that baseball must have rules to cover up the deficiencies of certain players. If we start protecting incompetence, where do we stop?

Schalk caught Big Ed Walsh, who had one of the best spitters any pitcher has yet to throw, legally or illegally. Ruel, who weighed in at 150 pounds including his glove, was Walter Johnson's battery mate. Johnson had a blazing fast ball which probably traveled faster than the delivery of any pitcher that came down the pike since the start of baseball. If little Muddy Ruel could catch "Big Train" Johnson, I can see no reason why modern-day catchers, standing over six feet and weighing 200 pounds, can't hold onto the butterfly knuckler.

Finley has a knuckle ball pitcher on his club named Tom Sturdivant, which explained his concern. I can't understand why the Kansas City catchers had trouble handling Sturdivant's knuckle ball, as the American Leaguers didn't seem to have too much trouble hitting it.

Finley and I slugged it out in the form of letters. Our battleground was the *Sporting News,* the baseball bible. The first blow:

FROM FRESCO TO FINLEY

Editor of The Sporting News:

I read with considerable interest the statements attributed to Charles Finley of the Kansas City Athletics regarding the decision of the Official Playing Rules Committee to outlaw the oversized catcher's glove.

I was busy on the floor of the convention and therefore was unable to take my place at the rules committee meeting in San Diego. Had I been there, I probably would have gone along with the majority of the committee.

I do resent the inference contained in Mr. Finley's statement that none of the committee members has a nickel invested in baseball. This is true, but entirely irrelevant. League presidents, umpires and managers do not have a nickel invested in baseball, but their decisions are of daily importance to the game of baseball.

While it is true I do not have any cash money invested in a ball club, I do have 42 years of my life invested in professional baseball as a player, manager, scout, farm director and club executive. I believe that this, in some degree, makes me more qualified to sit on the rules committee than an executive in the insurance field, no matter how successful the executive might be.

I wonder what type of rules committee we would have if the selection of its members was predicated on the amount of money each individual had invested in baseball?

Of all the things supposedly wrong with baseball, I firmly believe that the question of whether a few catchers are permitted to use a jai-alai player's cesta behind home plate belongs far down the list.

I remember an old saying that goes something like this: "Shoemaker, stick to your last."

> Fresco Thompson
> Vice-President, L. A. Dodgers,
> Los Angeles, Calif.

The counteroffensive:

FROM FINLEY TO FRESCO

Editor of The Sporting News:

I read Mr. Fresco Thompson's comments published in the December 21 issue of THE SPORTING NEWS, and it appeared to me that he missed my point entirely. Rule 25(c) of the Professional Baseball Rules (Organized Ball's administrative code) states, "Any Playing Rule may be revised, repealed or adopted by a majority vote of the Rules Committee, and the action of the Committee shall thereupon take effect."

As the Rules Committee is now constituted, it is an autonomous body whose agendas are secret and whose decisions are made unilaterally without regard for the opinions of management or ownership. This is inherently wrong and contrary to every concept of democratic action.

I know of no other group in this country, either in government, business or sports, that has dictatorial powers comparable to that of the Rules Committee.

The point I have been trying to make is simply this: The Rules Committee should extend to the manager and general manager the opportunity to express their opinions in regard to any proposed change, and any decision of the Rules Committee should then be submitted to the ownership of each league for ratification.

It seems only basic logic that individuals who have a financial interest in baseball should have a voice in any contemplated action that affects the game and therefore their investment.

Mr. Thompson stated that he remembered an old saying, "Shoemaker, stick to your last." If the so-called shoemakers (the owners) were to stick to their last, such as chewing gum, lumber, stocks and bonds, breweries, radio-TV, autos, insurance and other fields, Mr. Fresco Thompson would be out of a job. There would be no major league baseball. Mr. Thompson must still believe in Santa Claus.

CHARLES O. FINLEY
President of K. C. Athletics
KANSAS CITY, MO.

I would like to say in contradiction to Mr. Finley that the agenda of the Baseball Rules Committee is not secret; we are not the ones who propose rule changes; anyone, in or out of baseball, is privileged to do so and the Committee affords them all serious consideration. We receive suggestions from managers of semi-pro teams, high school coaches, college coaches, professional managers, and umpires.

Personally, I believe that the great charm of the game of baseball lies in the fact that the basic rules haven't been tampered with too much over the years.

I am not presumptuous enough to vote on an important rule change solely on my own judgment. I check with baseball people on the field and in the front offices in order to obtain a consensus of opinion before coming to a final decision.

I do believe in Santa Claus, but I don't believe the club owners wear red suits, have white beards, and are pulled by reindeer. Most of these gentlemen will give you all the birds you can catch. I have always, as a player, manager, and administrative officer, done a good day's work for a day's pay and I'm sure that if no major league ball existed, I and members of my family would have eaten regularly throughout the years. Baseball men, per se, did pretty well with their clubs over the years without outside money. I refer to such men as Charles Comiskey, Connie Mack, and Calvin Griffith. Comiskey built the Chicago White Sox into a valuable property, with his club generally in contention. Connie Mack won many pennants when the Athletics were a respected team in the American League. Griffith, although pressed for money with which to operate at times, did well with the Washington Senators.

Big business didn't become interested in major league baseball until it became big business—so they cannot take all the bows for its entity and present success.

CHAPTER 12

THE BATTLE OF CHAVEZ RAVINE

It was a twenty-five month delay after the Los Angeles City Council had voted ten to four, approving its contract with the Dodgers, that ground-breaking ceremonies were at long last held in Chavez Ravine. The date was October 19, 1959.

The two-year wait, fraught with a public referendum, an adverse Superior Court decision, two reversing actions by the State Supreme Court questioning the validity of our contract, a challenging State legislative bill vetoed by Governor Pat Brown, and physical eviction incidents, seemed a lifetime. And during the two years of bitter bickering and stalemate, labor and material cost zoomed.

Chavez Ravine had always been a haven for possums, jackrabbits, skunks, and squatters. It was littered with tin cans and populated by lovers at night. At night it looked desolate and cold as a clinical kiss under synthetic moonlight.

In 1938 plans were formulated to stage a World's Fair here. Had they been carried out, visitors might have asked: Which world is this? Later the Federal Housing Authority proposed to build $33,000,000 worth of apartments in the area. This was dropped. The City of Los Angeles purchased the property in 1951 with park and playground facilities in mind. Funds for such developments were not forthcoming.

Harold C. (Chad) McClellan, a paint manufacturer, was appointed by the City Council to negotiate with O'Malley. He was requested to negotiate, if he could, a meeting of minds somewhere within the general terms outlined in what later became known as the Arnebergh Memorandum, named after Roger Arnebergh, City Attorney. The City and County were prepared to make an offer containing the following provisions:

1. City and/or County to acquire and deed to the major league baseball club 350 acres in Chavez Ravine, including the present 257 acres now owned by the City, the additional acreage to be adjacent thereto. Such 350 acres to comprise an approximate circle, if possible.

2. City and/or County to provide access roads.

3. City and/or County to superficially pave parking areas.

4. City to accept dedication of circumferential roads.

5. The 350 acres, together with improvements, etc., to go on tax rolls.

6. There should be no deed restrictions on use of such 350 acres except that a modern major league stadium will be built and major league baseball brought to Los Angeles.

7. Major league baseball club, at its sole cost and expense, to build modern baseball stadium and bring major league team to Los Angeles.

8. Wrigley Field to be deeded to City and/or County in present condition as partial consideration for said 350 acres, with restriction against major league baseball being played in Wrigley Field.

9. Major league baseball club, as further consideration for said 350 acres, will agree to construct, maintain and make

available to the public, free of charge, various recreational facilities such as tennis courts, junior league baseball field, basketball courts, etc., these to be more specifically determined later.

10. As further consideration for said 350 acres, major league baseball club to agree to admit, at specified times, juveniles to ball games free, as an aid to the City and County in combating juvenile delinquency, etc.

Innumerable questions were discussed in the O'Malley-McClellan meeting. No commitments were made, but several points were clarified:

1. Contrary to impressions earlier given, a maximum of 306 or 307 acres could be made available at reasonable price in Chavez Ravine. 350 acres simply were not available.

2. A City reservoir on the property (within the area needed) must remain. Nor could the reservoir be moved or lowered. We must work around it or abandon the Ravine as a possible site.

3. Any plan contemplating land ownership by the Dodgers corporation must be developed on a legitimate buy and sell basis with values established fairly, in good conscience. There would be no free gifts or subsidy. McClellan explained—if we were planning to build a stadium and lease it to the Dodgers, considerable latitude would be permitted us. But he pointed out that O'Malley wanted to build a stadium and we didn't. Under these circumstances, regardless of our desires in the matter, we were forbidden by law to give 1 cent as an incentive to the Dodgers' transfer.

A specific proposal was made to the Dodgers on September 16, 1957.

1. The City will make available and convey to the Brooklyn National League Baseball Club a parcel of land consisting of about 300 acres, more or less, located in the Chavez Ravine area, reserving to the City one-half of the oil and

195

mineral rights and a suitable drill site and with the exception of 40 acres thereof as provided in Item 4 hereof.

2. The City will spend not to exceed $2 million for improvement of the site.

3. The Brooklyn National League Baseball Club will convey to the City the land and improvements known as Wrigley Field.

4. In the parcel mentioned in Item 1 hereof, 40 acres will be leased by the City to the Brooklyn National League Baseball Club for 20 years upon condition that the lessee construct and maintain thereon public recreational facilities to be designated by the City amounting to up to but not more than $500,000 construction cost and expend $60,000 per year for maintenance thereof. In the event that required maintenance does not amount to $60,000 in any one year the balance between such actual cost and $60,000 will be paid to the City for each such year. Upon faithful performance of such conditions herein set forth in Item 4 the City will convey to the Brooklyn National League Baseball Club said 40-acre parcel at the end of 20 years upon the same limitation as to oil and mineral rights provided in Item 1.

Suddenly the milk of human kindness that had been flowing toward the Dodgers in an undiminished stream became a mere trickle. Drops of poison were detected. A giant discussion whirled around the mineral rights in Chavez Ravine. Huge, rich deposits of uranium and cobalt were spoken of. I'm positive a Geiger counter could travel over every square inch of the Ravine without increased clickings. Rumor had it that enough oil was here to light every lamp in China.

O'Malley only wanted to play ball here—not dig for oil.

At any rate, a concession was made and the City reserved half the mineral rights. Thus far the only minerals turning up have been the fielding gems of the Davis boys.

Newspapermen, councilmen, sportswriters, sportscasters, and flannel-mouthed citizens got some exercise for the first time in years by jumping on and off the Dodger bandwagon. Unfortunately, no one broke a leg. However, regardless of how the wind was blowing from the storm center of Chavez Ravine, we had a number of staunch supporters in our corner, including Mayor Norris Poulson, Supervisor Ernie Debs, Councilwoman Rosalind Wyman, Councilman John S. Gibson, Jr., Vincent Flaherty and Mel Durslag of the *Los Angeles Examiner,* John B. Old of the *Los Angeles Herald-Express,* and Sam Balter, erudite sportscaster and columnist.

Balter delivered a stirring off-the-cuff speech before the City Council, of which I remember the windup:

"It will bring business and tourists with their golden dollars to the Golden West. This is a shift from the aging East to the growing West. It is progress. Don't let us down."

Once the plans for Dodger Stadium were submitted to city engineers for approval, obstacles appeared. No ball park had been built in the City since Wrigley Field, and that was constructed without rest rooms on the second level, an untold hardship to beer drinkers. We had almost as many city officials swarming over the park as we did contractors' workmen. You couldn't tell 'em without a scorecard.

Our connecting pipe to the city sewers wasn't large enough as a zoo was going to be located in Elysian Park, adjacent to the Stadium. Incidentally, the plans for the zoo now call for a location in Griffith Park, six miles from the Stadium.

We were required to have slot parking for all lots. This meant that each car would have its own slot from which it could leave at any time. This decision was made despite the fact that both the Coliseum and the Hollywood Bowl, two projects in which the City has a voice, allowed bumper-to-bumper parking.

If the lady of the house attends a game at Dodger Stadium and recalls she left the gas on the front burner of the stove going, she can climb into her car and drive from the park without a struggle. If the same situation exists at the Bowl or Coliseum, she might as well telephone the fire department to find out if her house is still standing. An alternative is to take a cab, which, in Los Angeles, can fracture the budget.

After spending nearly $22,000,000 in park improvements, we wind up with a conditional use permit. This restricts us to four events, over and above the playing of baseball, per month, but not more than two per week. Can you imagine stores in Los Angeles, such as Bullock's, The Broadway, Robinson's, or The May Company, building their stores with the understanding they would be permitted to sell tables, chairs, and beds every day in the week but could sell radios, TV sets, and table lamps only twice per week?

Dodger Stadium is the first baseball park built with private funds since the Yankee Stadium in 1923. The Yankee Stadium was built at a cost of $125 per seat, while Dodger Stadium's cost exceeds $400 per seat and we still aren't through.

San Francisco, Cleveland, Baltimore, Washington, Kansas City, Minneapolis, and Milwaukee use municipal stadia on which they pay no taxes, nor do they have tremendous sums tied up in a ball park. New York City has now built a new stadium for the Mets with City funds. The City of Houston is also building a park for its team. But Dodger Stadium is not only the most attractive ball park in the country, it's the first to be built with imagination. Heretofore contractors merely imitated other ball parks and added a few more seats—behind the same old posts.

The bulldozers that were to hack away at more than eight million cubic yards of earth for the Dodger Stadium ran into something more formidable than solid rock formations:

The Arechigas.

In 1951 when Chavez Ravine was under consideration as a federal housing project, the family of Manuel Arechiga began a fight against eviction. Their contention was that its property holdings were worth more than the $10,500 approved by the court. All legal steps to avoid ouster had been exhausted in 1953 when the City condemned their property. Since that time the Arechiga clan, housed in two dwellings, lived in Chavez Ravine without paying taxes.

The battle began on May 8, 1959, erupting into full-scale non-atomic warfare that was to split residents of Los Angeles into two hostile camps: against the Dodgers and for the Dodgers.

Captain Joe Brady of the Los Angeles Sheriff's Office, aided by a group of deputies and an eviction notice, pulled up before the Arechigas' houses with storage vans and bulldozers. Brady's object was simply to make the Arechigas comply with the law.

They had other ideas.

Armed with sharp teeth, long fingernails, their piercing screams sounding a battle cry, the Arechiga women and children swarmed to counterattack the enemy.

But before they could storm the Arechiga bastions,

deputies found the front doors of the two houses nailed shut. Arguments raged. An impasse developed. Inside the houses with their parents were the Arechigas' two married daughters, Mrs. Victoria Augustian and Mrs. Aurora Vargas, and seven children ranging from nine months to twelve years.

An emergency evolved. Diapers were needed. Victoria left the house. Deputies intercepted her. Fisticuffs began. In the midst of the melee three additional children arriving home from school sighted their mother fighting a male and a female deputy. They charged into the fray after dropping their school books. Aged five to seven, they swung their feet and fists at the deputies while their mother kicked, bit, gouged.

It took eleven minutes to subdue the tempestuous Victoria, who lasted longer than many opponents of Sonny Liston before she was handcuffed and her offspring removed to Juvenile Hall. Skirmishes continued inside the houses. At length the heads of the family, Abrana, sixty-nine, and Manuel, seventy-two, emerged of their own free will. Mrs. Arechiga carried a Chihuahua dog under each arm. After descending her steps, she deposited the dogs on the ground, picked up a rock and heaved it at a group of officers. Had she been Vero Beach-trained, her toss might have resulted in some cranial damage. As it turned out, no deputies were wounded.

The action took place only a block from the Police Academy where Los Angeles' finest are trained. Instructors here missed a good thing. The undergraduates should have been brought over to witness and given on-the-spot instruction on how to control a riot.

Once the last of the Arechigas was cleared off the property, the family from a distance witnessed bulldozers level their houses—houses that the City had condemned and demanded they vacate. There was no doubt they had vacated—the hard way.

The scarred deputies moved to the house of Mrs. Alice Martin, a seventy-three-year-old widow. She had previously warned them she was prepared to make a stand. However, she tossed in the sponge with a shrug of her aging shoulders the moment deputies demolished her barricaded doors.

The City had paid Mrs. Martin $24,000 for her property and $10,500 had long been on deposit with the county clerk for the Arechigas' holdings. They had never accepted the money. Mrs. Martin did.

The Arechigas promptly pitched camp for the night near the pile of rubble that had been their homes. The children bedded down in two cars, on a cot, and underneath an Army pup tent. A campfire burned throughout the night. No sanitation facilities existed. Attracted by TV pictures of the eviction, hundreds of curious persons arrived to mill around the Ravine. Many brought food which was piled on a card table. A huge coffee pot bubbled and gurgled, chorusing with the crickets.

Someone reported that just outside the flickering shadows of the campfire a beer party was held. Prompt denials followed.

"What is there to celebrate?" the Arechigas asked, gazing despondently at the razed dwellings.

City Health Officer George Uhl issued a statement: "The Arechigas must vacate their home in Chavez Ravine by May 12th. If they refuse we will order them to appear before the Health Commission to explain why. A tent is simply not a proper place to raise a family."

The day the embattled family was evicted, Howard

Holtzendorff, Executive Director of the Central Housing Administration, approached the Arechigas' daughter, Mrs. Mike Augustian, offering her a three-bedroom public housing unit, completely furnished, renting for $40 per month. The offer was refused.

"She told me they wouldn't take less than a house, and houses we don't have," Holtzendorff told newsmen.

Mike Augustian, a former boxer, gave another reason for turning down the offer. "They wouldn't let the Arechigas take along their chickens and dogs, and there weren't enough beds."

Holtzendorff denied this. "There would have been beds for everyone and they could have taken their three dogs along. It was impossible, of course, to let them keep 150 chickens in the middle of a public housing project."

Public sentiment favoring the Arechigas steadily mounted. O'Malley's character was again assassinated as it had been in Brooklyn and New York. Now he was pictured as an autocratic despot who attacks the helpless to throw them out of their homes. People thought of him, bullwhip in hand, forcing children and the aged to sleep in the chilled ravine.

A placard-bearing crowd of 300 thronged the City Hall chamber three days after the Arechiga eviction, to protest noisily what was called "an overt act." Some of the placards read:

WHO PUSHED THE BUTTONS THAT DEMOLISHED
THE HOMES IN CHAVEZ RAVINE?

WE REFUSE TO BE CHEATED OUT OF OUR LAND!

FAIR PLAY FOR THE ARECHIGAS!

A resolution was introduced by Councilman Karl Rundburg ordering Mayor Norris Poulson to appear at the public hearing and explain his position to those present.

The crowd, obviously supporting the Arechigas, was unruly and demonstrative. Councilman Edward R. Royball, often a champion of the "little man," had invited Abrana and Manuel Arechiga to appear before the Council to protest the destruction of the two houses the family was occupying just before the blast heard 'round the nation.

Victoria Augustian sobbed out her story before the gathering. Tears flowed like wedding wine. She charged that Councilwoman Rosalind Wyman was responsible for the eviction.

Her reasoning was slightly ambiguous.

"Mrs. Wyman is a mother and she must know how I feel and I want everyone to blame her because she is a woman."

The accusation—whatever the literal translation might be—prompted Councilman L. L. Timberlake to rise to Mrs. Wyman's defense by proclaiming, "The attack on her was unjustified and uncalled for."

Edward Royball, defender of the oppressed, was perhaps the most eloquent speaker on behalf of the Arechigas. He described the eviction as what you might have expected to find in Hitler's Germany or during the Spanish Inquisition.

The Council chamber rang with cheers.

A nephew of the Arechigas, Polin Cabral, mounted the rostrum, charging, "Walter O'Malley is taking this land for his own purposes. Councilmen here want to give away our property to the Dodgers. All my aunt and uncle want is what belongs to them, not charity."

Henry Lopez, lawyer, took up the challenge in describing what he saw in the Ravine. "It was most shocking. I saw parents and children literally bulldozed out of their homes."

And so the tempest grew in intensity, blown into hurricane proportions, scattering seeds of discontent over Southern California and prejudicing TV viewers. It ignited a prairie fire that crackled along out of control. One hundred years ago a lynch mob might have formed, and every Dodger executive be dangling at the end of a rope from a tree.

Then a big news story doused the fire and caused a return to sanity.

From the *Los Angeles Mirror-News*:

> The "homeless" Arechiga family, camping in a tent in Chavez Ravine, owns at least seven homes, the *Mirror-News* learned exclusively today. The Arechigas, center of a raging controversy since their eviction from two houses in the Ravine, rent out a majority of their houses.

It was later disclosed that the Arechigas owned eleven homes valued at $75,000, some of which were rental property. The bombshell came as a shock to thousands.

The disclosure was praised by Mayor Poulson. "The hypocrisy of this whole rigged demonstration has been exposed," he said. "Los Angeles has been nationally criticized due to the television program showing the evacuation of this family. The story by the *Mirror-News* ranks as one of the best public services I have ever seen since I have been Mayor. It's the type of journalism worthy of a Pulitzer Prize. The truth is now out in the open for all to see. Efforts have been made to show up the City as another Little Rock. While the truth is now out, the damage is done."

Thanks to some expert researching and reporting by the *Mirror-News,* the new avalanche of mud nearly inundating O'Malley was now washed off.

The Department of Public Works served the Arechigas notice that they must vacate their two tents in the Ravine. Manuel threw the notice on the ground. Policeman M. S. Pena, acting as a translator, picked up the notice, reading it in Spanish.

Television cameras were grinding, and as "the show must go on," there was a retake and this time the notice was handed to Abrana. She gave a more finished performance, taking violent action against the piece of paper —tearing it up, tossing the pieces on the ground, and spitting on them.

"This is my land!" she cried, facing the cameras. "You'll have to take us out dead!"

From mid-afternoon until nearly midnight the controversy raged. After a ninety-minute conference with Spanish-speaking Councilman Royball, the Arechiga family capitulated, agreeing to silently fold their tents and steal away from Chavez Ravine.

The campfires were extinguished. The show was over.

Mike Augustian expressed concern over moving the Arechigas' fowls. "The whole thing depends on getting chicken wire so we can take them with us," he said, adding, "You have no idea how hard it is to catch a rooster."

He should have said, "You have no idea how hard it is to catch an Arechiga."

Councilman Gibson remarked, "The blame rests

wholly with the anti-Dodger group and certain agitators who have a fetish for brewing trouble. Somebody put this family up to staying on the land that the City owned."

EDITORIAL *Los Angeles Times,* MAY 15TH 1959.

The real story of the Chavez Ravine episode has now been told, thanks to reporting in depth by the *Mirror-News* staff. When you look at the incident in perspective, its implications become more and more disturbing. They go far beyond the stage-managed resistance of the Arechigas family to a proper court order. You must face the fact that elected officials, sworn to uphold the law, actively condoned defiance of the law in the courts. Still other elected officials who did not participate in arranging this fraud on the public lost their heads and joined the hysterical attack on constituted authority.

It is clear now that the Chavez Ravine "victims" were "egged on" by some City Council members and certain powerful connivers who have spent large sums to keep the Dodgers out of this site. The residents of Chavez Ravine were "willing stars" in the disgraceful dramatics directed by these civic obstructionists. Unhappily a few television sensation mongers cooperated fully with the plotters who directed the scenario. They portrayed the far from homeless Arechigas as a destitute, tragic little family clinging in desperation to their humble cottage.

ALL THE SHABBY TRICKS

Every shabby, tear-jerking trick in the book was employed to create a wholly false impression of the wicked driving the meek out into the cruel world with a blacksnake whip. The *Mirror-News* exposed the fraud with the first story listing the Arechigas' extensive ownership of rental properties.

This in turn exposed a mawkish play for sympathy. Return of the Arechigas to a tent house—when they had a three-bedroom house a stone's throw away. The backstage managers of this melodrama showed no conscience about hoodwinking the local public and dragging the City's good name in the mud across the country via TV.

This was cold-blooded trickery. The anti-Dodger crowd knew that the Arechigas were under court order to move years before the Dodgers considered coming here from Brooklyn. They had been squatters on city-owned land for several years. Their land was condemned under the right of eminent domain. They were accorded due process of law. The court fixed the value of their land and the money was paid into the court. This is an orderly democratic process, necessary for the common good.

We would have no freeways, no sewers, no Bunker Hill project, no public utilities if needed land for them could not be condemned in the public interest. This was City-owned land from the day the decision became final. The Arechigas had no interest in it. They had no legal right to be there. That is the only point at issue.

Those who used them were guilty of an unwarranted dangerous attack on our system of government in advocating defiance of a lawful and finally adjudicated order of the courts.

MAJORITY WILL FLOUTED

We face a very serious situation in Los Angeles if a well-financed group, for whatever devious reasons, can flout the will of the majority of the people's elected representatives on City Council and obstruct the orderly processes of law. Then the safeguard planned civic improvements of our city will become a vast, deteriorating slum. Your home will decrease in value and no proper function of the city can be performed if rule-or-ruin fanatics can roadblock progress for any reason that occurs to a warped mind.

In complimenting the *Mirror-News* again, Mayor Poulson said, "While a number of television actors—I won't call them newspapermen—bled insincere tears up and down the picture tube without any effort to find out or present the true facts, the *Mirror-News* dug deeply into the story. The television actors who jumped to the Arechigas' defense competed with one or two of our City Councilmen for recognition as the greatest clowns of the year. Imagine this! Not one of these men, these bleeding hearts, made the slightest effort to find out the true need of the Arechigas or their true resources.

"But they did jump recklessly into the fight against the due process of law against the American heritage which we all hold so dear."

Attorney General Stanley Mosk praised Mayor Poulson for his stand after the disclosure. The Attorney General's letter said:

> I wish to commend you most enthusiastically for the splendid forthright statement that you made to television representatives concerning the Chavez Ravine matter. The spectacle created was a disgraceful reflection on the City of Los Angeles and those responsible for creating the illusion that public officials are ruthless when they enforce the law and court orders have done a disservice to our nation and its fundamental concept of justice.
>
> I'm delighted to see you express criticism of the television actors who so frequently distort the news and give emotional, slanted views in matters of public interest. The very same television actors whom you criticize, and everyone knows who they are, have assailed me, too, for adopting the same position which you and the City Attorney assumed in this case—that respect for our courts is essential if our American system is to survive. I wish that all public officials felt as keenly about this as you apparently do. Unfortunately, examples to the contrary may be cited in the Civic Center of Los Angeles.

The *Mirror-News* was named winner of the gold medal at the California State Fair for the top metropolitan news story of the year. The winning article was the exposé of the "homeless family" that held out in Chavez Ravine-Dodger Baseball Park eviction squabble.

Los Angeles Times, July 16th 1959

"Manuel Arechiga, 72, leader of the embattled family, was sentenced to five days in jail for drunk driving. He was also fined $259 by Municipal Judge David W. Williams."

I wonder what he was celebrating.

We were happy that the fight was over, but we weren't doing any celebrating. We had been sandbagged into paying half a million dollars for eight pieces of property which in total were valued at about $80,000.

CHAPTER 13

SOME ODDS AND ENDS

ONE of Walter O'Malley's worries—besides raising money—when the Dodgers made their westward move was what he called the "Hollywood influence." He spoke of the Dodger executives being a "happy family," and that while the phrase "going Hollywood" was vaporously defined, it did imply certain changes that he hoped wouldn't happen to any of us.

Buzzie Bavasi and I and others from the front office have never been caught in the vortex of so-called Hollywood life: the parties, the pursuit of cinema stars, the name droppings, or socializing with new friends from the movie colony. We still go to work in business suits and not sport shirts. We keep our distance from the "Dahling, you look terrific" set. Our wives walk into a room filled with people and leave without spectacular entrances and exitings.

None of the women in our group uses Gaborisms in conversation—bringing to mind the time Zsa Zsa walked into a restaurant where the wife of her former husband, George Sanders, was dining.

"Darling, what a divine hat," she complimented.

As she walked away from the table Zsa Zsa's companion reminded her, "She wasn't wearing a hat."

Zsa Zsa shrugged. "It really doesn't matter, darling."

We have often spoken of O'Malley's fears and laughed with him because among his close friends here are the Mervyn LeRoys, Mr. and Mrs. James Stewart, and the Jack Bennys, but the glitter of Hollywood could never pry O'Malley away from baseball. Dodger Stadium is his Taj Mahal. Here he is in business. Big business. Baseball business. The importance of this business was disclosed in a recent story released by the Los Angeles Chamber of Commerce in which they estimated that our failure to win the National League pennant in 1962 cost the city four million dollars in additional business. The hotels, restaurants, shops, and theaters were the heaviest losers.

The tears of these merchants, falling during one of our driest seasons, nearly raised the rainfall figures to normal for the year. I wonder where all these people who now profit from the Dodgers in Los Angeles were when we were looking for people to stand up and be counted? During those troublous times we needed every single friend we could find.

In a measure we stimulate employment in the city. While the players on the team are the main attraction, they form a very small part of the actual number of employees needed to put on our show. In the Dodger executive offices alone we have forty-seven employees. Seventy ushers and usherettes direct fans to their Stadium seats. There are fifty ticket sellers and fifty ticket takers. To preserve order in and around the Stadium, thirty special police are present, which should be enough to protect any umpire. A crew of sixty maintenance men must work for six hours to clean the Stadium after every game, often laboring through the entire night when a night game is followed by a day game. A ground crew of sixteen men is required to keep the playing field up to major league standards. These figures do not include the cashiers and parking attendants employed by the firm which has these concessions, nor the hundreds of vendors and counter people furnished by the ABC Vending Company who serve refreshments.

Two doctors and two nurses are always present. Forty maids and porters roam the park, keeping Dodger Stadium clean and comfortable. It costs us between $5,300 and $5,700 solely for park personnel to open the gates for a game.

I believe we are making a worthwhile contribution to the economy of the city, to say nothing of the general happiness spread when we beat the Giants.

The principal business in Southern California is still the tourist trade, despite the diversified interests locating here. A big-league ball club—especially if it's in the thick of the pennant fight—draws many of these people. Each day during the baseball season every daily newspaper in the country carries the dateline "Los Angeles" on its stories of the games played in Dodger Stadium.

The club and individual players have been the subject of feature stories in national magazines and on television shows. In Las Vegas you could even catch Maury Wills, Don Drysdale, Sandy Koufax, Tommy Davis, and Frank Howard in an act. Newspaper writers from principal cities come to the Stadium. During the play-offs against the San Francisco Giants for the pennant and the 1963 World Series, such nationally known syndicated sports columnists as Red Smith of the *New York Herald-Tribune,* Arthur Daley of the *New York Times,* Jimmy Cannon of the *New York Journal-American* and Dick Young of the *New York Daily News* filed stories headlined "Los Angeles." These men were only a few in comparison with other writers from principal cities in the United States. A major league baseball club brings a city news and publicity that no municipal agency could afford to purchase.

Never in the past has there been any glue invented or a common bond discovered that could unite the people of the hundreds of communities comprising the widespread Los Angeles area. Now they have a joint cause: the Dodgers. "Community Nights" allow the people of Anaheim, West Covina, South Gate, etc. a chance to meet their neighbors. Groups from various industrial firms enable workers to fraternize in a conclave of friendship, and cheer together.

None can say that the Dodgers don't generate excitement. I've head mousy office girls, who whisper "Yes, sir" and "No, sir" to bosses all day and lead dull lives of suppressed emotions, let their hair or wigs down and stand up and scream "Charge!" to the tones of the bugle. Previously, the only time they used that word was at a department store.

In Montebello two staunch Dodger fans, Joseph and his father Jerry Monte, lived in apartments one over the other. When the Dodgers and Giants were in their showdown series near the close of the 1962 season, plaster from the ceiling began falling on Joseph's head. Thinking it might be an earthquake, he ran upstairs to his father's apartment. Here he discovered the earthquake was man-made. Jerry Monte, following the game on radio, had stamped on the floor in his excitement when Wally Moon hammered out a hit.

The Dodgers have, as avid followers of our radio broadcasts, thousands of women, many of whom have scant knowledge of the game. My wife asked a market owner one afternoon when the Dodgers were playing in Philadelphia why there were so few persons in the store.

"Baseball," he said. "The women are home listening. The moment the game's over there'll be a rush."

The construction of Dodger Stadium removed an eyesore from the heart of downtown Los Angeles. Here in the center of gullies not level enough to play a game of two-handed gin rummy—much less a ball game—8,000,000 cubic yards of soil were moved, including cuts of 150 feet.

To give you an idea of the vastness of the project, one might visualize a building whose walls encompass a city block of 400 feet by 200 feet. If a building of those dimensions, and 260 stories high (the Empire State Building is eighty-five stories high), could be erected and filled to the top, it would then hold the earth and rock which had to be moved to create the site for the Stadium. Some 21,000 pre-cast units, weighing up to thirty-two tons, were poured and set in the outfield area, then lifted in the Stadium structural work.

In round figures—and I don't mean any of our individual fans—we have some 56,000 seats in Dodger Stadium providing an unobstructed view of one hundred per cent of the field thanks to the cantilever method of construction. There are seven front rows and no level is deeper than twenty-odd rows.

Forty-eight lounge and powder rooms—making it inexcusable for a lady to return to her escort with a shiny nose—are spotted about the park. The luxurious Stadium Club and a public restaurant with a sky-high view of downtown Los Angeles allow fans to come directly from their offices to the ball game.

Since the Dodgers came to Los Angeles, ten players presently on the Dodger roster have moved from their original homes and purchased houses in the city area. I don't believe that any other major league club has such a high percentage of its players making their homes in the city where they play.

The players enjoy living in Southern California. Better baseball weather doesn't exist. We've never had a postponement due to rain since moving here. Moose Skowron, whom we acquired from the Yankees and traded this year, was as sorry to leave Los Angeles as we were to see him go. Moose is a fine and popular gentleman. One reason he gave for liking it here was, "It's a relief to get away from the subways."

That reminds me of the time PeeWee Reese was captain of one of those great teams we had in Brooklyn. It was said that when Newcombe was pitching and Campy was catching, if Campy started out to have a conference with Newcombe, PeeWee would run at his fastest speed to get in on it because he loved the exchange of remarks between the battery mates.

He arrived at one of these mound meetings when Campy was berating Newcombe for not throwing hard and Newcombe innocently asked, "Campy, how can I throw hard if I can't throw hard?"

Campy returned, "Newk, you better do somethin' because when I signal for the express you throws me the local."

While it's true we have no expresses or locals running underground, we do have freeways. A freeway is an unofficial racetrack where human beings driving cars don't act human. People mention that the City of Los Angeles and the County spent in excess of $6,000,000 in access roads leading to the Stadium. In truth, some of these roads were needed in the area to expedite the freeway and freeway-access bottlenecks.

I'm certain that both the City and County would be delighted if every $6,000,000 they spent on roads and freeways throughout the Los Angeles area brought them an additional $400,000 in tax revenues.

That's a fair return on anyone's money. Almost as much as Billie Sol Estes promised on his investments.

Which brings us to the tax question.

At the very beginning O'Malley wanted to know how much his property tax would run. He was understandably concerned. I would guess that he had about $5,000,000 to invest. The rest would have to be borrowed. He couldn't possibly know that a stadium supposedly costing $10,000,000 to $12,000,000 would eventually cost $18,000,000 or more.

An estimate was made at $300,000 yearly on a 50,000-seat ball park. The tax on Ebbets Field in Brooklyn was $55,000. Soon after the legality of the Dodgers' contract with the City was challenged by forces unhappy with the deal, and O'Malley decided to expand the stadium to seat 56,000, tax estimates were altered to $345,000.

But the $345,000 figure was upped to $444,933 last year.

Today the assessment will run around $700,000.

Harold McClellan stated in a front page article in the *Los Angeles Herald-Examiner* written by Melvin Durslag: "As a negotiator, I am red-faced. I have lived in this area for fifty-one years and this is the first time I have been made to be ashamed of my home town.

"I have no personal tax quarrel with the Tax Assessor's office, but I do happen to know that the Dodgers have been deceived. We have waited until they have spent $18,000,000 on a luxurious ball park to hit them with taxes that violate the spirit of our original deal.

"O'Malley did not contest last year's assessment," McClellan continued. "He has no complaints about rising tax rates in the County. He is concerned only with unreasonable valuations placed on his land.

"I have similar concern, because I assured him that once we made an agreement he would have no cause for worry. I made a major point of telling him that we were the type of local government which would keep every promise. Under no circumstances would O'Malley have come to Los Angeles if he felt that he would have been taxed as he is today.

"Even if the tax had been justified at the time of our negotiation, he would have backed off because such an assessment for a baseball team is beyond the pale of economic tolerance."

So again in 1964 the Dodgers are fighting. This time it isn't just the Giants or the Cardinals, or perhaps Milwaukee or the Arechigas or the invisible enemies.

It's the great American fear: TAXES.

Chavez Ravine is once more shaping up as a battleground.

A war that we are certain will be fought here is the 1964 pennant race. Heavy hangs the crown of the World Champions! Every club in the National League is figuring out some way to dethrone us—some through trades to bolster weaknesses that became apparent during the 1963 season; others by releasing or trading veterans who slowed the team and replacing them by inserting into the lineups hungry, hustling youngsters.

It's my belief that the Dodgers are, again, the club to beat in 1964, despite our inability to trade for a fourth starting pitcher. In Koufax, Drysdale, and Podres, we have the best three-man rotation possible. In Perranoski and Miller we have a quality bullpen.

The Dodgers are primarily a young ball club. Few have reached the maturity plateau. The players are climbing toward their peak. From Pete Richert, Nick Willhite, Joe Moeller, and Phil Ortega can come an additional starter.

The chief threat will be the Giants. Opposing pitchers can get the shakes before they get to the park from just reading the newspapers to note the vicious batting order. Home run production for last year was: Willie McCovey 44, Mays 38, Orlando Cepeda 34. This is a gruesome threesome for any pitcher to challenge. The two catchers, Tom Haller and Ed Bailey, hit 35 round-trippers between them. No other club in baseball can pose the threat of having four positions in the lineup, each responsible for 34 or more home runs.

During 1963 the Giants' pitching was hurting with the collapse of Jack Sanford and Billy Pierce, who accounted for 40 wins for the 1962 pennant winners, but dropped off to a mere 19 victories last year. The Giants helped themselves where the pain was severest by securing pitchers Bob Hendley and Bob Shaw from the Braves in a winter trade.

It's mainly the acquisition of these two pitchers that causes me to feel the Giants stand squarely in the center of our pathway leading to the 1964 pennant.

In addition to the two pitchers, the Giants obtained the contract of Del Crandall. This gives them a right-hand-hitting catcher to spell the big left-hand-hitting Haller. Crandall is a field leader, something the Giants have lacked.

For the third spot in the standings, I must pick the St. Louis Cardinals, who made a fine run for top honors in 1963. The Cardinals traded with the Mets for "Hard Luck" Roger Craig in exchange for outfielder George Altman. Craig dropped 46 games for the Stengelites in the last two years. You have to be a pretty good pitcher for your manager to allow you to go to the post enough times to lose that many. The Cardinals hope that their better defense and stronger attack can make Craig, a former Dodger, reverse his Met won and lost record.

The Cards have a stellar infield. Bill White, Julian Javier, Dick Groat, and Ken Boyer are as fine a foursome as can be found. With the exception of Groat, they run with the speed of a relay team in track.

The trade for Craig, depriving the Redbirds of Altman, may come to haunt Manager Johnny Keane. They could ill afford to sacrifice an outfielder, being already thin in that department. This trade, combined with the retirement of amazing Stan Musial, leaves the Cardinals with one proven outfielder: the fleet center fielder Curt Flood. Now the right and left fielders must come from three youngsters who have yet to play a full season regularly in the majors: Doug Clemens, Mike Shannon, Charley James, and Johnny Lewis.

No club can lose a player of the prowess and stature of a Stan Musial without feeling pain. If I managed that club I'd have him sitting on the bench just as a morale builder, rubbing shoulders with the active players.

For the fourth position I have to select the young, eager Phillies of Manager Gene Mauch.

The Phillies also came up with a trade made with an American League club during the inter-league trading period. They gave up Don Demeter and pitcher Jack Hamilton for pitcher James Bunning and catcher Gus Triandos. The loss of Demeter will be seriously felt. The Phillies don't have too much right-hand hitting power.

The Demeter trade indicates the confidence the Phils have in rookie Richie Allen, who had an excellent year at Little Rock in the International League. He is said to possess a fine throwing arm, fast running speed, and good power at bat. With Johnny Callison, Tony Gonzalez, Wes Covington, and young Allen, the Phillies should have no concern over their outfield.

The addition of Triandos furnishes them with an experienced catcher who should prove invaluable to the embryo Philly pitchers. And on occasion Gus can hit the long ball.

The presence of Bunning adds balance to a pitching staff that was on the top-heavy side with youth and inexperience. I'm referring to Dennis Bennett, Ray Culp, Chris Short, and Dallas Green. Backed by this array, and Manager Mauch's spot-pitching of the veterans Cal McLish and Bunning, the Phils won't have to push many runs across the plate to be in the running. Also Jack Baldschun, Johnny Klippstein, and Ryne Duren are ready to step into relief when the regulars bog down.

Milwaukee, a fairly well-balanced club, seems destined for the fifth slot. Their trade with the Giants provides them with a left-hand hitting catcher to spell their excellent and youthful right-hand hitting receiver, Joe Torre. Felipe Alou brings Bragan speed and will strengthen the outfield, an Achilles heel of the Braves for several years.

I am apprehensive that the Milwaukee club might have thinned their pitching staff too much by trading off front line hurlers like Hendley and Shaw. Few clubs are so blessed with talent that they can trade pitchers of this caliber without striking a nerve.

On the Braves' roster are several young pitchers of whom Skipper Bragan is proud—namely, Larry Maxie, Wade Blasingame, Don Schneider, Arnie Umbach and Henry Fischer. If they fail to come through, the club may find the going tough. Tony Cloninger, Denny Lemaster, and Bob Sadowski might not be enough.

Of course, there's always ageless Warren Spahn. "He can't do it again," has been heard from year to year. But "Spahnie" does. Maybe this year he'll win 20 more.

The Cincinnati Reds look like a good sixth-place bet. At this writing, Fred Hutchinson, the manager, is fighting a malignancy, and those who know this colorful skipper—"the Bull of Crossley Field"—are praying he licks this latest enemy.

Cincy's pitching flopped in 1963. Bob Purkey and Joey Jay, victors in 44 games in 1962, sagged to a mere 13 wins in 1963. When a club has two of its aces hit such a toboggan, it's hard to get the sled back on the track again. Fortunately, big Jim Maloney and comebacker Joe Nuxhall picked up some of the slack.

The usually dependable Frank Robinson ran into the worst year of his career last year. His 1962 average of .342 dipped to .259 in 1963. If Robinson and a few other disappointments of last year bounce back, the Redlegs may move up a notch or two.

The Pirates may not rise above seventh place. Trades

didn't pan out. The loss of Groat, Dick Stuart's bat, and Don Hoak's steadying influence was insurmountable, coupled with the failure of Vernon Law to regain his old form.

On paper the pitching staff reads like world-beaters: Bob Friend, Don Schwall, Don Cardwell, Al McBean, Bob Veale, Joe Gibbon, and Carl Francis. It was their inability to settle on four regular starters that kept the club from clicking. In young Tommy Sisk the Pirates have come up with a jewel—a reliefer to help the aging Roy Face.

The fast-starting Chicago Cubs, who faded in the stretch, should nail down the eight spot. In the spring of last year excellent pitching by Dick Ellsworth, Bob Buhl, Larry Jackson, and Glen Hobbie and reliable bullpen work by Lindy McDaniel and Don Elston raised the hopes of Cub fans.

When your atomic weapon becomes a popgun, your attack fizzles, and that's what happened to Ernie Banks, a tower of strength for years. His batting average fell to a mere .227 and he dropped from 37 home runs to 18.

It will be Houston vs. the Mets for the dubious ninth and tenth place honors. Houston has the edge. Pete Runnels and the recently acquired Nellie Fox are the balance between the rookies and veterans. The Colts, short on power, have to scrape and scrounge for their runs, putting an extra burden on their pitchers.

The Mets are still the Mets, and the new park isn't going to change anything. They are competing with the Yankees for patronage and are forced to carry a couple of name players. Carrying some of the "people's choices" helps draw fans, but slowed down the progress of the club in the development of its youngsters.

I'm afraid that if the Met fans expect to enjoy the 1964 season, they had better spend most of their time inspecting the new park or watching the antics of Charles Dillon Stengel.

During last winter, Branch Rickey, now eighty-two, consultant on player personnel of the St. Louis Cardinals, was in Los Angeles. His mind still has the sharpness of a steel trap. The only physical change that I can notice in him through the years is his eyebrows. They are a trifle bushier and whiter, which gives Rickey more of an edge than ever in his player deals—something additional to hide his face behind when the old master dangles a low-paying contract.

The last player Rickey personally signed to a contract before departing from the Dodger organization was Johnny Podres. It was a wise choice, but it boomeranged. Podres beat the Cards the first game of a three-game series in St. Louis when the Cards were only half a game out.

It was the BIG one because it gave the Dodgers a psychological advantage and they went on to sweep the remaining two games.

"He killed our morale," Rickey admitted.

In an interview with Melvin Durslag of the *Los Angeles Herald-Examiner,* Rickey made the following observations on the Dodgers:

On Walter Alston: "He isn't a blowoff, but he won't be pushed off his doorstep."

On Buzzie Bavasi: "That fellow is a grass-cutter. He's out there mowing all the time."

On Leo Durocher: "No matter what they say, there are a lot of good things to that boy. If I owned control, I wouldn't be afraid to hire him to manage. But I admit there are times when you have to stay close to him."

Rickey had no statement to make about me. He may have a delayed one after reading this book. But he paid me an indirect compliment when he told Durslag, "The Dodgers are a prime example of a ball club home grown."

I like to think I helped cultivate that material.

CHAPTER 14

A PITCH AND A PRAYER

Reasons are numerous why the national game of baseball is an unpredictable sport. Foremost among these is that the cover of a baseball comes from the hide of a dead horse.

A live horse—as race track bettors tearfully attest—is an animal whose moods, whims, and caprices never guarantee its backers an old-age annuity. So that when wool yarn is wrapped over a cushion cork center under a piece of horse's skin that may have finished last in the eighth at Aqueduct, and stitched tightly by women workers of the A. G. Spalding plant at Chicopee, Massachusetts, then given to muscular young men to throw, catch, sometimes kick around, the unexpected can occur.

This is precisely what happened in the 1963 World Series when the Los Angeles Dodgers won an unprecedented four-straight victory over the terrors of the American League, the New York Yankees.

Sandy Kofaux went into the ninth inning of what was to be the final game with the Dodgers leading 2 to 1 in their own backyard. A year ago he had nearly lost a finger and a baseball career to amputation. On this pleasant, sunny afternoon, Yankee sluggers were swinging as if he had that same finger stuck in their eyes.

Bobby Richardson led off with a single. Tom Tresh struck out. Mickey Mantle watched a third strike zip by him. Elston Howard hit a ground ball to speedster Maury Wills on which he made a fine play and an off-balance throw to second, where apparently Dick Tracewski caught it to force the sliding Richardson.

Umpire Tom Gorman jerked his thumb skyward, indicating an out and the end of the game. Koufax's facial mask of tenseness cracked into a wide grin as he jumped into the air from the mound to show his delight. He started off the field.

His move was premature. The ball squirted from Tracewski's glove. Gorman reversed his decision, spreading his arms. The runner was safe. The ball was returned to Koufax, who slammed it disappointedly into his glove, hitched up his pants, and began concentrating on Hector Lopez, the next batter.

Lopez grounded to Wills, who tossed to Moose Skowron on a reprieve play, forcing Howard at second.

The Dodgers under Manager Walter Alston were the World Champions!

Koufax now really put on a jump. It was high enough to clear his $13,000 players' share of the series if the bills had been stacked in fives on the infield. It was understandable that Koufax jumped higher than any winning pitcher under similar circumstances. Koufax, like all jumpers, had first taken a practice leap. He established a new height record to go with his fifteen strikeouts in the first game at Yankee Stadium.

A far cry from a collection of sluggers—they had the

lowest batting average of any team winning the pennant for the last eighteen years—the transplanted Brooklynites, enjoying superb pitching from Sandy Koufax, Don Drysdale, Johnny Podres, and reliefers Ron Perranoski and Bob Miller, plus fleetness on the base paths, overall spirit, and a few prayers, had stormed to the National League pennant.

Now with the close of the final World Series game at Dodger Stadium in Chavez Ravine the long, long season had officially ended. The married players could return to their wives, lounge around the house, and perhaps plan for the birth of future ballplayers—especially those slated for salary increases in 1964.

Players, club officials, press, radio, and television people swarmed into the Dodger clubhouse. Champagne flowed. Hands were shaken. Backs were thumped. Congratulatory cries split the air. Bob Miller, acquired from Casey Stengel's tail-end club in a winter deal which sent Tim Harkness and Larry Burright to New York, was shouting, "I'm the first Met to make the World Series."

Relaxed before the NBC mike, sipping a glass of champagne, Sandy Koufax, who resembles a good-looking edition of night-club comic Ben Blue, was asked his immediate plans.

"To take a shower," he answered laconically.

Vin Scully, who has boomed the sales of transister radios throughout the sprawling Los Angeles area and is probably worth more at the box office than any single player on the Dodger roster, stood atop a trunk, inviting both players and club officials to help make the TV wrap-up.

Tom Gallery, sports director of NBC, nudged me.

"Come on, Fresco, I want you to say a few words."

"Okay," I replied.

227

His eyebrows raised. "Was that your voice I just heard?"

"It's what's left of it after four games," I replied.

"Well," he said, "it'll be the first time television had any static."

I fought my way to the trunk. It was worse than a freeway jam leading to the stadium. Standing on the trunk was a man-made mountain—Frank Howard, 255 pounds, six feet seven inches. Dwarfed underneath his leg spread, with my five foot eight height I didn't look much like a club executive. I looked more like a piece that fell off Howard.

Howard was born in Green Bay, Wisconsin, and how Vince Lombardi ever let a future Packer such as big Frank slip away from the town is a mystery that Erle Stanley Gardner couldn't solve. In the first game at Yankee Stadium, Howard hit a tremendous drive off Whitey Ford that crashed against the dead-center field fence some 460 feet from home plate.

Old-timers recalled that they had never seen a ball clouted so far there, including efforts by Babe Ruth, Lou Gehrig and Mickey Mantle. One of these days Howard will unleash a line drive at the opposing pitcher and the only identification left on the mound is going to be a laundry mark.

Near the end of the season Frank decided he was going to show what he'd learned from Wills about base running by trying to steal second. He thundered in, jarring the whole stadium as he struck the ground to begin his slide.

I called our switchboard and instructed one of the operators, "If Cal Tech telephones to say their seismograph has discovered an earthquake in the vicinity of Chavez Ravine, just tell them Nature had nothing to do with it."

When Howard climbed down from the trunk after concluding his TV stunt, I said a few words which I'm sure weren't understood, and then retreated to a corner of the room to watch the festivities. Champagne was being poured by the players over one another, the uniforms, suits of clothes, as if someone from a cleaning establishment encouraged the activities.

We'd only been able to defeat the nearly invincible Yankees once in six previous World Series. By conquering them in four straight we now felt that we'd squared accounts with the fellows who used to be our cross-town rivals in New York.

I'd been a member of the Dodger organization since 1931, but I felt that this was, beyond question, the highlight of my career to watch men of assorted ancestries, creeds, religions, and skin pigmentation become jubilant brothers in a rising crescendo of joy.

We were then the only team in the majors with two Jewish boys—Sandy Koufax and Larry Sherry—who was sold this year. This inspired comic Phil Silvers to comment, "The Yanks promptly signed a petition demanding that Yom Kippur be celebrated the first week in October."

There are plenty of capable Jewish athletes, but they always seem to veer away from baseball. It's puzzled me. Hoping to discover why this was the case, I posed the question to Hank Greenberg:

"Why aren't there more Jewish boys in organized baseball?"

"Did you ever see a Jew who likes to step on a diamond?" Hank retorted.

I still don't know.

Our champions of 1963, helped by the base thievery of Maury Wills and Willie Davis (the latter described by

Vin Scully, "when he runs it's all downhill"), were vastly removed from the teams of yesteryear known as the "Daffiness Boys."

Only in the third game of the World Series was there a hint of a throwback to this screwball era. This was when Johnny Roseboro and Tracewski found themselves together on third base, as if seeking an introduction.

Johnny has a great sense of humor, aptly illustrated the time he requested on the Dodger passboard: TWO TICKETS FOR GOV. ROSS BARNETT. BAD SEATS PREFERRED.

I'm sure, though, he didn't think it very funny when both he and Tracewski stood on the same bag.

In contrast to the joy of the Dodgers, the Yankees in their dressing room were not singing in the showers, although most bathers, having just learned from the IBM machines that they were $8484 richer from the losers' share, might have been humming a few bars from "You Are My Sunshine."

For one of the defeated Yankees, Elston Howard—had he but known—a shower was unnecessary. Here at Dodger Stadium we have automatic sprinklers, set for one hour after the game to water the outfield. The New Yorkers were gloomingly heading for their bus, parked in center field, when the water geysered forth, dousing the lagging Howard.

Feeling badly about this, I dropped Elston a note expressing our regrets at his having received his second shower and stating that it was purely accidental. I hope he believed me.

That evening, custom prevailing, we held a victory party in our Stadium Club to which players, their wives, club officials, scouts, and the press were invited. Earlier we had advised our membership of 750 that the Club would be closed to them after a certain hour. Consequently, they did their celebrating early.

Before we dined Monsignor Patrick Gallagher, who had married Mr. and Mrs. Walter O'Malley in Brooklyn, gave the blessing. It was then that I remarked to those around me, "We ought to observe a moment of silence for those people who paid scalpers $50 to $100 per ticket for Monday's game and will now turn them in for a $12 refund."

It was a night to be remembered.

When a World Series is to be played in any city a spreading fever infects thousands of people whose interest in baseball may have lain dormant for many years. A man who takes an exploratory trip to his attic to stumble upon a mildewed catcher's mitt purchased from the defunct A. J. Reach and Company, Philadelphia, believes the discovery entitles him to a World Series ticket.

Few realize that each participating club has obligations to other clubs in the National and American circuits, to the Commissioner, to League presidents, to season box holders—all of which results in a scarcity of public tickets. The World Series does not particularly belong to each of the competing clubs; it is under the supervision of the Commissioner of Baseball, and no passes are available.

But that doesn't stop the public from trying.

In Fullerton, where I live, Mrs. Thompson never got better service while shopping than she did ten days prior to the Series. Butchers gave her choice cuts of meat. Extra trading stamps just happened to drop into her shopping bag. People inquired after my health who the week before wouldn't have lost a second's sleep if I were the victim of bubonic plague. Friends we saw only at Christmas parties began telephoning. Then, exactly one week before the Series opened, these same solicitous people made their opening pitch. It never varied, "Now, understand, I don't want a pass. I want to pay for the tickets."

A few days before the first game in Los Angeles I needed a haircut, which I decided to postpone, as sports fans generally congregate in barbershops. As my hair wasn't so long that it would hang over my eyes, impairing vision, I decided to wait.

Letters began pouring in.

I received one from a player, formerly connected with our organization and now living in Pennsylvania. There was nothing timorous about him. He wrote that he wanted four passes for the first game in Yankee Stadium. I told him so would I, but, unfortunately, I was going to have to pay $12 for my tickets just like everyone else.

Two letters saved for future laughs were:

"Dear Mr. Thompson:

Remember the time when you were a freshman at George Washington High School in New York and we played 'Spin the bottle?' After we kissed you said you'd never forget it. I'm trusting your memory and would like two tickets for the second game at Yankee Stadium."

I answered:

"My memory has become faulty after 46 years."

"Dear Mr. Thompson:

I used to hold you on my knee when you were a mere baby and everybody said I was the same as a 'second mother' to you. Could you favor me with four tickets to the first game at Yankee Stadium—box seats preferred?"

232

I wrote:

"If you held me on your knee, as you claim, then you must be getting on in years. Therefore, I don't think it would be wise to expose yourself to the dangers encountered in a crowd."

Another Manhattan dweller guessed I might not remember him too well, but stated that I once had a fight with his cousin when we both were attending P. S. 186. He said that since his cousin and I had been so close, would I be kind enough to send him six passes to either or both games at Yankee Stadium.

In a letter postmarked "Brooklyn," the writer concluded his note with, "By sending me passes it will help atone for your treachery in aiding our team to leave our city."

The telephone rang constantly. Everyone was trying to get into the act. One gentleman pleaded, "What am I going to have to do, climb that flagpole in center field in order to see the Series?"

I told him, "Maybe you will if you get there early enough, because I understand the line is already forming."

My first name, Fresco, is an odd one, and I am sometimes called Fresno or Crisco or Frisco by mistake. I don't enjoy the "Frisco" tag. It awakens sore memories of what the Giants did to us in the stretch drive of 1962. Many of the moochers who telephoned and addressed me by one of these wrong names, pretending to know me intimately, made it easy to say no.

I think the funniest phone call of all was made by a woman to Buzzie Bavasi.

"Mr. Bavasi," she said, "I don't know whether or not you remember me, but I was your partner for a Halloween party at Scarsdale when we were eight years old. Of course we were wearing masks at the time."

I had a good friend who is mayor of a midwest city. He wrote me for a strip of tickets, which I sent him and he paid for. When a scalper was arrested and we traced the seized tickets, they turned out to be His Honor the Mayor's. All I can say is that maybe the City Council should vote him a pay raise.

When the chairs tilt back and the feet of ruralites go up on the hot stoves during winters of the future to re-hash the surprising brevity of the 1963 World Series, before feet start smoking, accolades should be paid to our Director of Scouting, Al Companis. Al, born in the Dodecanese Islands, is the only Greek in organized baseball. There's an old saying: "The Greeks had a word for it." Not in Al's case. He had many words for it, a voluminous number, neatly inscribed and filed under the heading: NEW YORK YANKEES. In this project Al had two aides-de-camp: Lefty Phillips and Ted McGrew.

Companis camped on the Yankees' doorstep three solid weeks to learn who stole bases, who bunted, who hit-and-run, who had a good arm, bad arm, what pitchers used what, pitchers you could steal on, wait out, etc.

"It was the most comprehensive scouting report I've ever seen," complimented Bavasi.

Examples of samples:

"Pitch curves to Clete Boyer." Result: One hit for Boyer in thirteen times at bat.

"Joe Pepitone has a weak arm." Result: Jim Gilliam sped from first to third when a throw slipped by Pepitone.

"Johnny Blanchard never hits to the left of second base." Result: On a crucial play in the fifth inning of the second game, Wills was in perfect position to field Blanchard's grounder.

"Detected a give-away move by Tony Kubek, indicating the hit-and-run play was on." Result: Drysdale picked Kubek off first base in the third game.

This may bring forth a question. Why do you need a scouting report on players who have been in the majors for years? The answer is that some hitters change. They go from being strong high-ball hitters to strong low-ball hitters. They may at first have difficulty connecting with inside pitches; then outside pitches. They've been thrown so many pitches to their weaknesses that, being real major-league caliber pros, they overcome these deficiencies.

Speaking of hitting reminds me of the time we were finishing up with a tryout camp when one of the tyro players came to me for advice. He said, "Mr. Thompson, I wonder if you could help me with my hitting?"

"Son, what's your problem?" I inquired.

He explained, "I always seem to be hitting under the ball. I just hit little fly balls."

"Hmmm," I mused. "Just how much do you think you're hitting under the ball?"

He held up his thumb and index finger, separated a quarter of an inch.

"Son," I said gravely, "my recommendation is for you to go to a dime store and get yourself a pair of inner soles just about the thickness you indicated. They'd raise you exactly enough so that instead of hitting just under the ball you'd now be hitting in the middle of it."

Later I relented and showed him how to overcome his difficulties without buying inner soles.

When Al Companis returned from his microscopic examination of the Yankees, I asked him, "Do they hit many pop flies?"

He looked at me as if I were a refugee from a nut house. "Pop flies? Who keeps track of pop flies?"

"I think you should have, Al," I said in a serious voice. "You should have paid special attention to that, because you as well as I know that's been our weakness all season —too much of the 'Alphonse and Gaston' politeness... 'Never the Twain Shall Meet' in the field."

Al shook his head and, muttering to himself, walked away.

As with other phases of baseball, scouting has undergone alterations. In the old days there were no farm systems. The name "farm" was taken literally. It meant a tract of land devoted to the raising of domestic animals or crops—not a spawning ground for the training of baseball players trying to crash the Big Time.

There was no extensive scouting. The major-league clubs had one scout east of the Mississippi and one scout west of that river. Now we have them for the east and west side of any main street in a sizable city. All you have to do is stretch out your throwing arm in any direction and you're liable to touch one. If you attend a high-school game along the Atlantic Seaboard, those older men seen in the stands, who nearly outnumber the spectators, are not over-age students who flunked and are trying to graduate. They're scouts.

Why, today I'm afraid I'll open my mail and find that one of my scouts has signed another scout for lack of something else to do. That's how prolific they've become.

I have some advice to tender fathers with sons of fourteen, fifteen, or sixteen years of age who want their offspring to become play-for-pay baseball athletes. Just send him into a sporting goods store to buy a glove. The moment he beats his fist into it and looks at all as if he understands the gesture, somebody'll jump up from behind a showcase and sign him to a contract. Perhaps even a bonus.

The Dodgers, paralleling the movement of other teams, dissolved rapidly after the World Series. The next monumental event was when Bavasi mailed out the 1964 contracts.

Walter O'Malley left on an African safari.

Walter Alston returned to his place of birth—Darrtown, Ohio—saying, "I just want to sit on a log with my grandson and shoot squirrels." Walt can afford plenty of ammunition. His 1964 contract was $52,500.

Financial offers poured in for the playing heroes. Tommy Davis, Drysdale, and Koufax displayed new skills on TV network programs and made public appearances.

Koufax, voted the Most Valuable Player of the Year, was presented with a car by *Sport Magazine*. Commented Maxwell Styles, sports editor of the *Hollywood Citizen-News:*

"He had to beat a Ford to get a Chevrolet."

When it came time to speak, Sandy sang the praises of the Yankees. "We were fortunate. We did everything right for four days. They still have a great team, and we respect them for it.

"We wanted to beat them for one reason: we wanted to be World Champions. We'd heard about their $3,000,000 infield. As far as I'm concerned, it is. Tony Kubek and Bobby Richardson amazed me at the double plays they made when I thought there was no chance. Clete Boyer has to be as good as any third baseman in the game today. Joe Pepitone is a great first baseman who had a fine year and helped them win the pennant.

"We're proud we won. They have nothing to feel ashamed of. They won a pennant, which takes a lot of doing, day after day for five and a half months. But we won four games using only thirteen men. That's an amazing thing."

Asked how he felt when Dick Tracewski dropped the throw at second base, Koufax smiled. "I had two great thrills in the World Series;" he said, "when I thought it was over, and then when it actually was over."

The usual cry heard around the nation of "Break up the Yankees!" wasn't heard any more. The Dodgers had done just that.

It had to be the sports story of the year.

With virtually the same team our stars might not sparkle as brightly in 1964. Nothing is certain in baseball.